THE
SLOW COOKER
BIBLE

Publications International, Ltd.

Favorite Brand Name Recipes at www.fbnr.com

Pictured on the front cover *(clockwise from top right):* "Peachy Keen" Dessert Treat *(page 302),* Chicken with Italian Sausage *(page 108),* Sweet Chicken Curry *(page 142)* and Fiesta Black Bean Soup *(page 220).*

Pictured on the back cover *(clockwise from top):* Slow-Cooked Kielbasa in a Bun *(page 164),* Mixed Berry Cobbler *(page 280)* and Turkey with Pecan-Cherry Stuffing *(page 112).*

ISBN-13: 978-1-4127-2334-3
ISBN-10: 1-4127-2334-5

Library of Congress Control Number: 2005927784

Manufactured in China.

8 7 6 5 4 3 2 1

Preparation/Cooking Times: Preparation times are based on the approximate amount of time required to assemble the recipe before cooking, baking, chilling or serving. These times include preparation steps such as measuring, chopping and mixing. The fact that some preparations and cooking can be done simultaneously is taken into account. Preparation of optional ingredients and serving suggestions is not included.

contents

The Joy of Slow Cooking

The slow cooker is one of the most popular appliances in today's kitchen—and for good reason. What other appliance allows you to start dinner in the morning, then gives you the freedom to enjoy your day far from your kitchen? And, when you arrive home a hot savory dinner is waiting. You can easily take a slow-cooked dinner to a potluck supper and keep it warm during serving. When entertaining you can rely on your slow cooker to free up a burner or leave valuable oven space for another item on your menu. Plus, cleanup is quick and easy. No wonder slow cookers are loved by cooks across America.

The information that follows is designed to help you get the most from your slow cooker. You'll learn what they do best and why. Discover important techniques that can produce more flavorful dishes or help you create low-fat meals. Learn the tricks to cooking rice, pasta, fish and baked goods like cakes and breads. And you'll understand how to safely prepare foods at home and transport them. Finally, this book is packed with 200 taste-tempting recipes your family is sure to love. From easy appetizers and hearty main dishes to hot soups, spicy chilis and even desserts, this book has a fabulous collection of winning recipes and valuable information.

Don't wait any longer to get started on a quick course in slow cooking. Soon you'll be putting all your new knowledge to work to prepare family-pleasing meals every day of the week.

Slow Cooker Basics

A Little Bit of History

The introduction of the slow cooker: The first electric slow cooker was introduced in 1971. It was a more versatile variation of an electric bean pot. Available in only one size, 2½ quarts, it was similar in appearance and operation to today's models.

In the 1960's women in the United States were joining the work force in huge numbers; for the first time family cooks were away from home many days of the week. It suddenly became important to find ways to quickly get dinner on the table after work. The maker of the first slow cooker saw the need and responded with an appliance that, surprisingly, didn't prepare dinner quickly, but rather it cooked dinner slowly while the cook was off pursuing her career. When the energy crisis occurred not long afterward, sales skyrocketed. The energy-efficient slow cooker was a huge hit.

The rebirth of the slow cooker: After its first brush with popularity, the slow cooker lost favor as other options were presented to cooks. A variety of frozen and shelf-stable meals became available and fast food restaurants multiplied. Although its popularity

waned, a group of determined home cooks continued to love the appliance and used it frequently. In the mid 1990's the slow cooker began a slow comeback, aided by the introduction of slow cooker cookbooks with contemporary recipes. With their newly found popularity, slow cookers began to appear in more and more kitchens, at potluck suppers and on buffet tables. Manufacturers responded with variations on the original slow cooker: more sizes, more features and more creative ways to use them.

Popularity: Slow cookers remain popular in the twenty-first century for many reasons. First and foremost, they are easy and convenient to use. The concept is simple: cooking slowly at a temperature high enough for food safety but low enough that the cook doesn't need to attend to it for long periods of time. Busy cooks appreciate one-dish meals because they require little attention, cleanup is quick and everyone loves the food.

How Does a Slow Cooker Work?

Basic concept: A slow cooker is usually a metal container with a heavy ceramic insert. Inserts have either a clear glass or plastic cover. Most inserts are removable for easy cleaning.

There are two general types of slow cookers. The most common type has heating coils that circle the outer container producing heat on either a low or high setting. The low setting is generally about 200°F and the high setting is about 300°F. Food is placed in the insert, covered and heated by the slow steady heat produced by the coils. The recipes in this book were developed and tested with this type of slow cooker. The second type has heating coils under the insert that cycle on and off. The recipes in this book have not been tested with this type of appliance, so refer to the manufacturer's directions for help.

The slow cooking process creates steam. Since the slow cooker is covered throughout the cooking process, the steam can't escape. Instead, it condenses to form liquid that returns to the food. The amount of liquid in the food increases during cooking, so don't be surprised if there doesn't seem to be enough liquid when you begin cooking.

Slow cookers require very little energy, making them economical to use. In addition, they don't heat the kitchen, so they are a good choice for cooking on hot summer days.

What they do best: Slow cookers are ideal for making soups, stews and chilis, dishes that require long cooking. Slow cooking allows flavors of the meat or poultry and vegetables to develop and blend. Long slow cooking tenderizes meat. Choosing less tender cuts of meat is wise and you'll save money because tougher cuts are often more economical.

Other uses: Slow cookers are useful when entertaining. When used to prepare one of the dishes on the menu, a slow cooker will free up a burner or space in the oven for something else. And the slow-cooked dish gives you more time to concentrate on other menu items. A slow cooker can also be used to keep foods hot on a buffet table. Whether it's hot mulled cider, a warm artichoke dip or a main dish, your slow cooker can save the day.

Prepare your favorite slow-cooked dish and carry it to a potluck dinner. (Special carriers are made for just this purpose.) Desserts, such as fruit dishes, puddings and custards, can be prepared in a slow cooker. Surprisingly, even cakes can be made in this appliance. You'll find that these cakes are moist, because they've been steamed. They can be made right in the ceramic insert or in a special cake pan offered by one manufacturer. Pudding cakes, moist cakes with pudding underneath, also work well in a slow cooker.

Don't try this at home: Since a slow cooker uses low temperatures, it can't be used for sautéing or deep-frying. Nor can it be used to cook a large quantity of pasta. Leftovers should never be reheated in a slow cooker. For safety's sake, leftovers need to be reheated quickly (see Slow Cooker Safety, page 19 for more information).

There are electric cookers available that do many things besides slow cooking. If you're looking for greater versatility in one appliance—steaming, boiling, deep frying and slow cooking—do research at a retail dealer that carries small appliances or on the Internet. These units have heating coils on the bottom of the unit. The recipes in this book have not been tested in this type of unit, so rely on the manufacturer's directions to guide you.

Choosing a Slow Cooker

It's important to know how you plan to use a slow cooker before shopping for one. For everyday cooking, choose a size large enough to serve your family (see the chart below). If you plan to use the slow cooker primarily for entertaining, choose one of the larger sizes. The 16-ounce size is great for keeping dips hot. This unit has only one heat setting, low.) If you're new to slow cooking, consider choosing a basic unit. They can be found for under $20 at discount stores. You can always upgrade later. Some cooks find owning more than one slow cooker useful.

Sizes: Basic slow cookers range in size from 16 ounces to 6½ quarts; they can be either round or oval in shape. Round slow cookers are more common and generally less expensive; oval units

Slow cooker size	Number of servings
1½ quarts	1 to 2
2½ quarts	2 to 4
3 quarts	3 to 4
3½ quarts	3 to 5
4 quarts	4 to 6
5 quarts	4 to 6
6½ quarts	6 to 8

can more easily accommodate large pieces of meat. Choose the appropriate size from the chart above. Most recipes in this book require a 2½- to 3½-quart slow cooker.

Features: Features available on some slow cookers include keep-warm settings, programmable timers, delayed-start settings, fast-start settings and countdown timers. There's even a model that has preprogrammed settings for a host of specific recipes. If you need even greater flexibility than most slow cookers, look for a unit that has a ceramic insert that has been designed to handle extreme temperatures; the insert can be used on the range top and in the oven. Keep in mind that the more features a model has, the higher the price.

Extras: Accessories for slow cookers include travel carriers, storage covers, meat racks and baking pans.

Slow Cooker Techniques

If you have never used a slow cooker, the following techniques will help you get started and give you a clear understanding of the world of slow cooking. If you're an old hand at slow cooking, browse through the list of techniques and you might find the solution to a problem you've experienced. Or, you might discover something new that will enhance your slow-cooking experience and turn you into an expert.

Tenderizing: Since slow cooking is an effective way to tenderize meat, tougher cuts of meat, which have more flavor than lean cuts, are an excellent choice. Many of the recipes in the "Hearty Meat Dishes" chapter include cuts like brisket, chuck roast, rump roast, stew meat, pork spareribs and pork shoulder. But the selection isn't limited to just these cuts; you'll find some of the convenient choices you love, such as flank steak, ground beef, sausage and pork chops.

Preparing meat: It is best to trim meat and poultry of excess fat before cooking, because the fat will liquefy and float to the top and you'll need to skim it off after cooking. You may wish to brown meat in a skillet before adding it to the slow cooker (see Browning below).

Browning: While not necessary, browning meat does have benefits. You've probably noticed that searing meat on a grill or in a skillet produces wonderful aromas and distinctive flavors that make steaks, burgers and chops extra special. The flavor produced by browning will add complexity to slow-cooked beef, pork and lamb meals. Ground meat should always be browned and drained of fat before placing it in the slow cooker. Browning also gives meat a more pleasant color.

Preparing poultry: Chicken skin tends to shrivel and curl in the slow cooker, so most recipes call for skinless chicken. If you prefer to use skin-on pieces, brown them in a skillet before adding them to the slow cooker. Remove excess fat from poultry before cooking it. A whole chicken is too large to cook safely in a slow cooker; always cut whole chickens into quarters or individual pieces before cooking.

> If you prefer, you can purchase skin-on chicken for greater savings. To remove the skin easily, simply grasp the skin using a paper towel and pull it away from the meat.

Preparing vegetables: Vegetables, especially root vegetables, can take longer to cook than meats. Cut vegetables into uniform pieces so they finish cooking at the same time. Root vegetables, like potatoes, carrots and turnips, should be cut into small pieces and placed on the bottom of the slow cooker so they are always covered with liquid. Vegetables should not be precooked. Occasionally a recipe will call for sautéing onions and garlic; this is usually done to reduce their sharpness. For example, in Classic French Onion Soup (page 194), the onions are sautéed for 15 minutes to allow them to develop a caramelized flavor, which adds a very distinctive note to the finished soup.

Strong-flavored vegetables, such as broccoli, cabbage and cauliflower, should be added during the last hour or two of cooking. Shorter cooking prevents their flavor from overwhelming the dish. Tender, delicate vegetables, such as spinach, green onions and snow peas, should also be added during the last hour of cooking to prevent overcooking them.

Dairy products: Long, slow cooking (6 hours or more) can make dairy products curdle or separate. Add milk, cream, sour cream and cheese during the last 15 to 30 minutes of cooking.

Certain dairy products can be used successfully during long cooking because they have undergone high heat processing. Examples of these are processed cheese and evaporated milk, which can be safely added early in the cooking process. Condensed soups can also withstand long cooking.

Boosting flavor: When foods cook for a long time, dried herbs and some spices tend to diminish in flavor, resulting in a bland dish. As more steam condenses in the slow cooker and the liquid in the dish increases, flavors become diluted. (Conventional cooking, on the other hand, results in evaporation of liquid and seasonings tend to become stronger the longer they are cooked.) To correct this problem, always taste the dish about 30 minutes before the end of the cooking time and add additional herbs and spices as needed.

On the other hand, some spices and garlic increase in flavor. The best examples of this are chilies, chili powder and pepper, which can become very harsh and extra-spicy during long cooking. If you or a family member is sensitive to heat from chilies and spices, use less than the recipe suggests or wait until the last 30 minutes to add it.

The flavors of fresh herbs will increase during long cooking, making fresh herbs a good choice for slow cooking.

Improving color: Long cooking can result in vegetables losing their bright color. Finished dishes may look washed out. To avoid this problem, add delicate vegetables near the end of cooking. Another option is to garnish the dish before serving. Colorful garnishes like chopped green onions, chopped herbs, chopped fresh tomatoes, shredded cheese, lemon or lime wedges, and crisply cooked and crumbled bacon add just the special touch needed. Sour cream, toasted nuts and croutons also add interest. Be sure that the flavor of the garnish complements rather than detracts from the dish.

Make-ahead preparation: Mornings can be hectic times. If time is at a premium in the morning in your kitchen, you may find it easier to prepare ingredients the night before. For safety's sake, cover and refrigerate all items until ready to use. Also, keep vegetables in a separate bowl from raw meat and poultry. Do not brown meat or poultry the night before; partially cooking meat or poultry and refrigerating it allows bacteria to grow. Add the prepared ingredients to the slow cooker; you may need to add an extra 30 minutes to the cooking time because the ingredients will be very cold.

Filling the slow cooker: For best results, fill the slow cooker insert at least one-half full, but not more than three-quarters full. Many recipes recommend

placing firm root vegetables on the bottom of the insert and the meat on top of the vegetables.

High versus low: Slow cookers have two settings, low and high. Most recipes can be cooked at either setting. Generally, 2 to 2½ hours on low equals 1 hour on high. Most of the recipes in this book give cooking times for both low and high settings. If the recipe only lists one heat setting, this is the only one that should be used. Cooking on the low setting may result in slightly better blending of flavors and tough meats may become more tender when cooked on the low setting.

Start high, finish low: Another option for slow cooking is to cook for the first hour on the high setting, then reduce the heat to low to finish the dish. This reduces the total cooking time by one to two hours. Some slow cooker models offer a feature that automatically changes the heat setting to low after 1 hour on high.

Keep the lid on: A slow cooker can take as long as 30 minutes to regain the heat lost when the cover is removed during cooking. Only remove the cover when instructed to do so in the recipe. Generally, slow cooker dishes seldom, if ever, need stirring. With heating coils wrapped around the outside of the appliance and low heat, there's no danger of scorched food.

If you can't resist the urge to peek in the slow cooker, simply tap the cover gently or spin it lightly to remove some of the condensation. You should be able to see what's going on in the slow cooker.

Thickening: Thickeners are usually added during the last 15 to 30 minutes of cooking. The amount of liquid created in a slow cooker dish may vary from unit to unit. Cooking on the low heat setting or for a longer time results in more juices than cooking on high. Removing the lid repeatedly during cooking will reduce liquids. If there doesn't seem to be much liquid, use only a portion (one-half to three-fourths of the listed amount) of the thickening agent, adding more if necessary. If the sauce becomes too thick, simply thin it with additional broth or water.

There are four thickening

agents that can be used in slow cookers. The two most common are flour and cornstarch.

Flour: All-purpose flour is most often used in the recipes in this book. Place the flour in a small bowl or cup and stir in enough cold water to make a thin, lump-free mixture; a whisk can help eliminate lumps. With the slow cooker on the high setting, quickly stir the flour mixture into the liquid in the slow cooker. (Remove large pieces of meat or poultry from the slow cooker before thickening the liquid.) Cook, stirring frequently, until the mixture thickens. Instant flour may be substituted; it can be stirred directly into hot liquid.

Cornstarch: Cornstarch gives sauces a clear, shiny appearance; it is used most often for sweet dessert sauces and stir-fry sauces. Place the cornstarch in a small bowl or cup and stir in cold water, stirring until the cornstarch dissolves. Quickly stir this mixture into the liquid in the slow cooker; the sauce will thicken as soon as the liquid boils. Cornstarch breaks down with too much heat, so never add it at the beginning of the slow cooking process. And as soon as the sauce thickens, turn off the heat.

Arrowroot: Arrowroot (or arrowroot flour) is a ground powder of a tropical root; it produces a clear sauce. Those who are allergic to wheat often use it in place of flour. Place arrowroot in a small bowl or cup and stir in cold water until the mixture is smooth. Quickly stir this mixture into the liquid in the slow cooker. Unlike cornstarch, arrowroot thickens below the boiling point so it can thicken sauces easily with the low heat of a slow cooker. Too much stirring can break down an arrowroot mixture, so be sure and use it just before serving. (See the Substitution chart on page 23 for information on substituting arrowroot for flour.)

Tapioca: Tapioca is a starchy substance extracted from the root of the cassava plant. It comes in many forms but it is the quick-cooking form that is used in several recipes in this book. Its greatest advantage is that it withstands long cooking, making it an ideal choice for slow cooking. Add it at the beginning of cooking and you'll get a clear thickened sauce in the finished dish. Dishes with tapioca as a thickener are best cooked on the low setting; tapioca may become stringy when boiled for a long time.

Low-fat techniques: One great advantage of slow cookers is that you can easily prepare low-fat meals in them. Since foods are not generally sautéed in butter or oil, the fat content is naturally lower in slow cooked meals. To trim even more fat from slow cooker dishes, choose lean meat, trim excess fat, remove the skin from chicken and brown meat in a nonstick skillet lightly sprayed with nonstick cooking spray. Or, slip meat under the broiler for a few minutes to brown it before adding it to the slow cooker. Any fat that does accumulate during cooking will rise to the surface and can be skimmed off.

Baked goods in a slow cooker: If you wish to prepare bread, cakes or pudding cakes in a slow cooker, you may want to purchase a covered, vented metal cake pan accessory for your slow cooker. You can also use any straight-sided soufflé dish or deep cake pan that will fit into the ceramic insert of your unit. Baked goods can be prepared directly in the insert; they can be a little difficult to remove from the insert, so follow the recipe directions carefully. (See Foil handles technique below for tips on removing soufflé dishes and cake pans from your slow cooker.)

Doubling recipes: Generally, when doubling a recipe, double the amount of meat, vegetables, herbs and spices. (See page 11 for spices that increase in flavor; don't double these. Instead, make adjustments near the end of the cooking time.) Only increase liquid ingredients by 50 percent. Refer to your owner's manual for additional instructions.

High altitude adjustments: If you live at an altitude above 3500 feet, you will need to make some adjustments when slow cooking. Everything will take longer to cook, so plan for that. Tough meats take longer to tenderize at high altitudes, sometimes much longer; try cooking on the high heat setting instead of low. Root vegetables take longer to cook as well; cut them into smaller pieces than the recipe suggests for quicker cooking.

Foil handles: To easily lift a dish or a meatloaf from a slow cooker, make foil handles as shown below.

Tear off three 18×3-inch strips of heavy-duty foil. Crisscross the strips so they resemble the spokes of a wheel. Place the dish of food in the center of the strips.

Pull the strips up and over the dish or food; using the foil handles, lift the dish or food and place it into the slow cooker. Leave the strips in during cooking so you can easily lift the item out again when it's ready.

Slow Cooker Techniques for Special Foods

Frozen foods: Avoid cooking frozen foods in a slow cooker. For food safety's sake, do not cook frozen meat or chicken in a slow cooker. Instead, thaw it in the refrigerator before cooking. It's best not to cook packages of frozen vegetables in a slow cooker; rather, thaw them or cook them conventionally or in a microwave oven. You may add small amounts (½ to 1 cup) of frozen vegetables, such as peas, green beans, broccoli florets and corn, to a slow-cooked meal during the last 30 to 45 minutes of cooking. Cook on the high setting until the vegetables are tender. (You may need to add a few minutes to the cooking time.)

Rice: Choose converted long-grain rice (or Arborio rice when suggested) or wild rice for best results. Long, slow cooking can turn other types of rice into mush; if you prefer to use other types of rice instead of converted rice, cook them conventionally and add them to the slow cooker during the last 15 minutes of cooking. You can add a small amount (½ cup) of uncooked rice to a slow cooker soup or other dish; be sure to add it to boiling liquid during the last

hour of cooking and cook on the high setting. (You may need to add a few minutes to the cooking time.)

If you wish to add rice to a recipe that doesn't include it, you will need to adjust the liquid as well. Add an equal amount of water or broth before you add the rice.

Pasta: Pasta needs to be cooked in a large quantity of boiling water; it should not be cooked in a slow cooker. However, you can add small amounts (½ to 1 cup) of small pasta, such as orzo, small shell macaroni, ditali and short lengths of linguine to boiling liquid during the last one hour of slow cooking. You may also cook pasta in boiling

water and add it to the slow cooker during the last 30 minutes of cooking.

Fish: Fish cooks quickly and can easily be overcooked. That's why it requires special care when slow cooking. First, choose only firm white fish, such as cod, haddock, sea bass, red snapper or orange roughy. Avoid more delicate varieties and thin fillets because they will fall apart. If fish is frozen, thaw it overnight in its original packaging before cooking it.

Add the fish 30 to 45 minutes before the end of the cooking time. Change the heat setting to high before you add the fish, cover the slow cooker and cook until the fish just begins to flake when tested with a fork. The cooking time is dependent upon the quantity and the thickness of the fillets—the thicker the fillets and the more of them, the longer they take to cook.

Shellfish: Shellfish, such as shrimp, are delicate and should be added to the slow cooker during the last 15 to 30 minutes of the cooking time. Always use a high heat setting for shellfish. If you add a large quantity of shellfish to the slow cooker, you may need to add a little extra cooking time. Watch shellfish carefully; it overcooks easily.

Dried beans: It's best to presoak dried beans before cooking them in a slow cooker. This softens them and gives them a head start on cooking. Softening beans reduces the cooking time. (Lentils and split peas do not need to be softened.) The two methods for presoaking follow:

Traditional method: Place dried beans that have been sorted and rinsed in a bowl. Cover them with cold, unsalted water and let them stand overnight. Drain off the water and place the beans in the slow cooker.

Quick method: Place sorted and rinsed beans in a large saucepan; cover them with twice their volume of cold unsalted water. Bring the water to a boil over high heat. Boil for 2 minutes. Remove the saucepan from the heat, cover it and let it stand for 1 hour. Drain off the water and place the beans in the slow cooker.

Even when beans are presoaked, they take a long time to cook. Avoid adding acids or sweeteners to the beans until they are soft. Acids and sweeteners will slow down the softening process and will lengthen the cooking time. Acids include tomatoes, vinegar and citrus juices. Sweeteners include sugar, honey and molasses. Add these items toward the end of the cooking time.

Fondue: A small slow cooker (1½ quarts) makes a perfect stand-in for a fondue pot. Whether you want to make a cheese fondue or a chocolate dessert fondue, the low heat of a slow cooker ensures perfectly melted cheese or chocolate in 45 minutes to 1 hour.

Adapting Recipes to the Slow Life

You can adapt many of your favorite conventional recipes to the slow cooker. Choose recipes that are normally prepared on top of the stove, such as soups, stews, chilis and braised meats and poultry; they tend to adapt better. Find a similar slow cooker recipe to use as a guide. Note the cooking times, amount of liquid, quantity and size of meat and vegetable pieces. Because the slow cooker captures moisture during cooking, you will want to reduce the amount of liquid by one-third to one-half.

Follow the techniques suggested in the previous pages for meat, poultry, vegetables, cheese, rice, pasta, seasoning and thickening. Make sure the

If your converted recipe has too much liquid, you can scoop out the excess and discard it. Or, you can remove the excess and place it in a saucepan; simmer it until the mixture is reduced by at least half. This technique is called "reducing" and it reduces the liquid while intensifying flavors. Add the reduced liquid back to the slow cooker.

the slow cooker is at least half full (see page 12) You may find you need to experiment a little to get the proportions correct.

Caring for Slow Cookers

Cleaning: Cleaning your slow cooker is actually pretty simple. Refer to the tips that follow for basic guidelines.

• Always wash a new ceramic insert in hot sudsy water before cooking in it. It may have a film on it from the manufacturing process.

• For sticky foods like barbecued ribs and other foods containing sugary ingredients, spray the insert with nonstick cooking spray for easier cleanup.

• After cooking, wash the cool insert in hot sudsy water.

• To remove any sticky food, soak the insert in hot sudsy water, then scrub it with a plastic or nylon scrubber. Do not use steel wool.

• Wipe the cool outer container with a damp cloth.

Extreme temperatures: Ceramic inserts are sensitive to sudden changes in temperature. Don't place a cold ceramic insert into a preheated base. Don't place a hot insert on a cold surface, in the refrigerator or fill it with cold water. Unless the manufacturer's directions say you can use the ceramic insert in a conventional or microwave oven, don't. Finally, never place the ceramic insert in the freezer.

Slow Cooker Safety

Food safety: Food safety is always a concern when you're cooking and serving food. Organisms that cause food-borne illness thrive at temperatures between 40°F and 140°F. Research has shown that slow cookers, even on the low heat setting, raise the temperature of the food quickly through this danger zone, making them a safe way to cook.

Power outage: If you arrive home and find the electrical power service to your home is out, check the slow cooker immediately. With an instant-read thermometer, check the temperature of

the contents of the slow cooker. If the temperature is above 140°F, you can transfer the contents to a large saucepan or Dutch oven and finish cooking it on a gas range or gas grill. However, if the temperature of the contents is between 40° and 140°F, you should throw the contents away.

If the electricity is on when you arrive home, but you can tell by the clocks that your home has been without power, the best thing to do is throw away the food.

You will never know what the temperature of the food was when the power went off or how long it was off; the food may have spent several hours in the danger zone. And, although the food is hot when you get home and looks done, it is better to err on the side of safety and throw it away.

Make-ahead safety: When you prepare ingredients ahead for later cooking, always refrigerate meat and vegetables. Store raw meat and poultry in a separate bowl from the vegetables. Do not store ingredients in the slow cooker insert; starting with a cold insert will lengthen the cooking time.

Frozen foods: Do not cook frozen meat or poultry in the slow cooker. It takes too long on either the low or high setting to go through the danger zone, which gives organisms a perfect place to grow and multiply. Frozen vegetables are best prepared on the range top or in a microwave oven.

Browning: Never brown or partially cook meat or poultry, then refrigerate it for later cooking. Instead, cook it immediately after browning.

Cook meat and poultry thoroughly: At the end of the cooking time, check the temperatures of poultry, meat and meatloaf using an instant read thermometer. Poultry should be 180°F, beef and pork 160° to 170°F and meatloaf 165°F.

Warm setting: Some slow cookers have a warm setting that is designed to hold food above 145°F. You can confirm that your slow cooker is working properly by checking the temperature of the food periodically while it is on the warm setting. The temperature should not drop below 140°F.

Leftovers: Refrigerate leftovers quickly. Food can stand in a slow cooker that is turned off for up to 1 hour. To quickly chill leftovers, divide them into several small containers rather than one large container; they will chill faster and bacteria will have less chance to multiply. Never reheat leftovers in a slow cooker. Instead, heat them quickly on the top of the range or in a microwave oven.

Filling the slow cooker: A slow cooker that is less than half full may not heat food quickly enough. Since the heating coils circle the outer container, most of the food will not be in contact with the heat source.

Appliance safety: Slow cookers are safe to leave unattended while they are cooking. If you plan to be away

from the house all day, it is safer to leave the slow cooker on the low setting. Do not use your slow cooker near the kitchen sink. Choose an electrical outlet at least three feet from the sink. Never immerse the base unit in water. Do not use the ceramic insert if it is cracked; replace it. For further safety tips, refer to the manufacturer's instructions.

Electrical cords: Protect the electrical cord from nicks and cuts. Check the cord periodically; if you find nicks or cuts in the cord, replace it. Do not use an extension cord with a slow cooker.

Slow Cooker Pantry

A well-stocked pantry can make slow cooking even more convenient. Having frequently used items on hand means you can prepare dinner without a special trip to the supermarket. The following items are often used in slow cooker recipes. Customize the list so you can prepare your favorite recipes any time.

Canned chicken and beef broth	Pasta	Brown sugar
Condensed cream soups	Converted long-grain rice	All-purpose flour
Canned diced tomatoes	Dried herbs	Cornstarch or arrowroot
Tomato sauce	Vegetable oil	Evaporated milk
Tomato paste	Olive oil	Onions
Dried beans	Nonstick cooking spray	Garlic
Canned beans	Granulated sugar	Boiling potatoes

Keep your refrigerator stocked with your favorite slow cooker vegetables and dairy products.

Carrots

Celery

Bell peppers

Milk

Sour cream

Cheese

Keep a small assortment of frozen meat, poultry and vegetables in the freezer.

Lean ground beef* (1-pound packages)

Beef stew meat*(1-pound packages)

Chicken pieces* (packages of 4 pieces)

Boneless chicken breasts* (packages of 2 breasts)

Green peas

Green beans

Corn

Stew vegetables

Meat and poultry have limited storage time in the freezer. Use ground beef within 3 months, stew meat within 6 months and poultry within 8 months. If you don't use these packages of meat and poultry for slow-cooked meals, be sure and use them for something else before they lose quality. Always thaw meat, poultry and large quantities of vegetables before cooking them in a slow cooker (see "Frozen foods" page 16).

Ingredient Substitution Guide

If you don't have:	Use:
Arrowroot (1 tablespoon)	2½ tablespoons all-purpose flour
Baking powder (1 teaspoon)	¼ teaspoon baking soda plus ½ teaspoon cream of tartar
Bread crumbs (1 cup)	1 cup cracker crumbs
Broth, chicken or beef (1 cup)	1 bouillon cube or ½ teaspoon granules mixed with 1 cup boiling water
Butter (¼ cup or ½ stick)	¼ cup margarine or 3½ tablespoons vegetable oil
Cheddar cheese (1 cup shredded)	1 cup shredded Colby or Monterey Jack cheese
Cornstarch (1 tablespoon)	2 tablespoons all-purpose flour
Ricotta cheese (1 cup)	1 cup small curd cottage cheese
Cream or half-and-half (1 cup)	1½ tablespoons melted butter plus enough whole milk to equal 1 cup
Garlic (1 small clove)	⅛ teaspoon garlic powder or ¼ teaspoon garlic salt
Ketchup (1 cup)	1 cup tomato sauce plus 1 teaspoon vinegar and 1 tablespoon sugar
Lemon juice (1 teaspoon)	½ teaspoon vinegar or 1 teaspoon lime juice or white wine
Lemon or orange peel, fresh (1 teaspoon)	½ teaspoon dried peel
Mayonnaise (½ cup)	½ cup sour cream or plain yogurt
Milk, evaporated (1 cup)	1 cup light cream
Mushrooms, fresh (½ pound)	1 can (4 ounces) mushrooms
Mustard, prepared (1 tablespoon)	1 teaspoon dried mustard
Onions, minced (¼ cup)	1 tablespoon dry minced onion
Asiago or Romano cheese, grated (½ cup)	½ cup grated Parmesan cheese
Dried cranberries (1 cup)	1 cup raisins
Saffron threads (½ teaspoon)	½ teaspoon turmeric
Sour cream (1 cup)	1 cup plain yogurt (not low-fat)
Tomato juice (1 cup)	½ cup tomato sauce plus ½ cup water
Tomato sauce (1 cup)	⅜ cup (6 tablespoons) tomato paste plus ½ cup water
Vinegar (1 teaspoon)	2 teaspoons lemon or lime juice
Wine (1 cup)	1 cup chicken or beef broth or 1 cup fruit juice mixed with 2 teaspoons vinegar

Appetizers & Snacks

Chunky Pinto Bean Dip

2 cans (about 15 ounces each) pinto beans, rinsed and drained
1 can (14½ ounces) diced tomatoes with green chilies, undrained
1 cup chopped onion
⅔ cup chunky salsa
1 tablespoon vegetable oil
1½ teaspoons minced garlic
1 teaspoon ground coriander
1 teaspoon ground cumin
1½ cups (6 ounces) shredded Mexican cheese blend or Cheddar cheese
¼ cup chopped cilantro
Blue corn or other tortilla chips
Assorted raw vegetables

1. Combine beans, tomatoes with juice, onion, salsa, oil, garlic, coriander and cumin in slow cooker.

2. Cover; cook on LOW 5 to 6 hours or until onion is tender.

3. Partially mash bean mixture with potato masher. Stir in cheese and cilantro. Serve at room temperature with chips and vegetables.   *Makes about 5 cups dip*

Prep Time: 12 minutes
Cook Time: 5 to 6 hours

Chunky Pinto Bean Dip

Honey-Mustard Chicken Wings

3 pounds chicken wings
1 teaspoon salt
1 teaspoon black pepper
½ cup honey
½ cup barbecue sauce
2 tablespoons spicy brown mustard
1 clove garlic, minced
4 thin lemon slices

1. Rinse chicken and pat dry. Cut off wing tips; discard. Cut each wing at joint to make two pieces. Sprinkle salt and pepper on both sides of chicken. Place wing pieces on broiler rack. Broil 4 to 5 inches from heat about 10 minutes, turning halfway through cooking time. Place chicken wings in slow cooker.

2. Combine honey, barbecue sauce, mustard and garlic in small bowl; mix well. Pour sauce over chicken wings. Top with lemon slices. Cover; cook on LOW 4 to 5 hours.

3. Remove and discard lemon slices. Serve wings with sauce.

Makes about 24 appetizers

Prep Time: 20 minutes
Cook Time: 4 to 5 hours

Helpful Hint

Browning chicken before cooking it in a slow cooker serves several purposes: browning contributes a pleasant flavor as well as color to the chicken wings.

Honey-Mustard Chicken Wings

Creamy Artichoke-Parmesan Dip

2 cans (14 ounces each) artichoke hearts, drained and chopped
2 cups (8 ounces) shredded mozzarella cheese
1½ cups grated Parmesan cheese
1½ cups mayonnaise
½ cup finely chopped onion
½ teaspoon dried oregano leaves
¼ teaspoon garlic powder
4 pita breads
Assorted cut-up vegetables

1. Combine artichokes, cheeses, mayonnaise, onion, oregano and garlic powder in slow cooker; mix well.

2. Cover; cook on LOW 2 hours.

3. Meanwhile, cut pita breads into wedges. Arrange pita breads and vegetables on platter; serve with warm dip. *Makes 4 cups dip*

Cranberry-Barbecue Chicken Wings

3 pounds chicken wings
Salt and pepper
1 container (12 ounces) cranberry-orange relish
½ cup barbecue sauce
2 tablespoons quick-cooking tapioca
1 tablespoon prepared mustard
Hot cooked rice (optional)

1. Preheat broiler. Rinse chicken and pat dry. Cut off and discard wing tips. Cut each wing in half at joint. Place chicken on rack in broiler pan; season with salt and pepper. Broil 4 to 5 inches from heat for 10 to 12 minutes or until browned, turning once. Transfer chicken to slow cooker.

2. Stir together relish, barbecue sauce, tapioca and mustard in small bowl. Pour over chicken. Cover; cook on LOW 4 to 5 hours. Serve with hot cooked rice, if desired.
Makes about 16 appetizer servings

Prep Time: 20 minutes
Cook Time: 4 to 5 hours

Creamy Artichoke-Parmesan Dip

Slow Cooker Cheese Dip

1 pound ground beef
1 pound bulk Italian sausage
1 package (16 ounces) pasteurized processed cheese spread, cubed
1 can (11 ounces) sliced jalapeño peppers, drained
1 medium onion, diced
8 ounces Cheddar cheese, cubed
1 package (8 ounces) cream cheese, cubed
1 container (8 ounces) cottage cheese
1 container (8 ounces) sour cream
1 can (8 ounces) diced tomatoes, drained
3 cloves garlic, minced
Salt and pepper

1. Brown ground beef and sausage in medium skillet over medium-high heat, stirring to break up meat. Drain. Transfer to 4-quart slow cooker.

2. Add processed cheese, jalapeño peppers, onion, Cheddar cheese, cream cheese, cottage cheese, sour cream, tomatoes and garlic to slow cooker. Season with salt and pepper.

3. Cover; cook on HIGH 1½ to 2 hours or until cheeses are melted. Serve with crackers or tortilla chips. *Makes 16 to 18 servings*

Helpful Hint

Processed cheese can better withstand long slow cooking. Since it's processed with heat and has emulsifiers added, it will remain smooth and creamy.

Slow Cooker Cheese Dip

Spicy Sweet & Sour Cocktail Franks

2 packages (8 ounces each) cocktail franks
½ cup ketchup or chili sauce
½ cup apricot preserves
1 teaspoon hot pepper sauce

1. Combine all ingredients in 1½-quart slow cooker; mix well. Cover; cook on LOW 2 to 3 hours.

2. Serve warm or at room temperature with cocktail picks and additional hot pepper sauce, if desired.   *Makes about 4 dozen cocktail franks*

Prep Time: 8 minutes
Cook Time: 2 to 3 hours

Chili con Queso

1 package (16 ounces) pasteurized processed cheese spread, cut
   into cubes
1 can (10 ounces) diced tomatoes with green chilies, undrained
1 cup sliced green onions
2 teaspoons ground coriander
2 teaspoons ground cumin
¾ teaspoon hot pepper sauce
   Green onion strips (optional)
   Hot pepper slices (optional)
   Tortilla chips

1. Combine cheese spread, tomatoes with juices, green onions, coriander and cumin in slow cooker; stir until well blended.

2. Cover; cook on LOW 2 to 3 hours or until hot.

3. Garnish with green onion strips and hot pepper slices, if desired. Serve with tortilla chips.   *Makes 3 cups*

Serving Suggestion: For something different, cut pita bread into triangles and toast them in a preheated 400°F oven for 5 minutes or until they are crisp.

Spicy Sweet & Sour Cocktail Franks

Barbecued Meatballs

      2 pounds 95% lean ground beef
1⅓ cups ketchup, divided
      3 tablespoons seasoned dry bread crumbs
      1 egg, lightly beaten
      2 tablespoons dried onion flakes
      ¾ teaspoon garlic salt
      ½ teaspoon black pepper
      1 cup packed light brown sugar
      1 can (6 ounces) tomato paste
      ¼ cup reduced-sodium soy sauce
      ¼ cup cider vinegar
1½ teaspoons hot pepper sauce
      Diced bell peppers (optional)

1. Preheat oven to 350°F. Combine ground beef, ⅓ cup ketchup, bread crumbs, egg, onion flakes, garlic salt and black pepper in medium bowl. Mix lightly but thoroughly; shape into 1-inch meatballs. Place meatballs in two 15×10-inch jelly-roll pans or shallow roasting pans. Bake 18 minutes or until browned. Transfer meatballs to slow cooker.

2. Mix remaining 1 cup ketchup, sugar, tomato paste, soy sauce, vinegar and hot pepper sauce in medium bowl. Pour over meatballs. Cover; cook on LOW 4 hours. Serve with cocktail picks. Garnish with diced bell peppers, if desired.

Makes about 4 dozen meatballs

Barbecued Franks: Arrange 2 (12-ounce) packages or 3 (8-ounce) packages cocktail franks in slow cooker. Combine 1 cup ketchup with sugar, tomato paste, soy sauce, vinegar and hot pepper sauce; pour over franks. Cook according to directions for Barbecued Meatballs.

Barbecued Meatballs

Parmesan Ranch Snack Mix

3 cups bite-size corn or rice cereal squares
2 cups oyster crackers
1 package (5 ounces) bagel chips, broken in half
1½ cups small pretzel twists
1 cup pistachio nuts
2 tablespoons grated Parmesan cheese
¼ cup (½ stick) butter, melted
1 package (1 ounce) dry ranch salad dressing mix
½ teaspoon garlic powder

1. Combine cereal, oyster crackers, bagel chips, pretzels, nuts and Parmesan cheese in slow cooker; mix gently.

2. Combine butter, salad dressing mix and garlic powder in small bowl. Pour over cereal mixture; toss lightly to coat. Cover; cook on LOW 3 hours.

3. Remove cover; stir gently. Cook, uncovered, 30 minutes. Store snack mix in airtight container. *Makes about 9½ cups snack mix*

Prep Time: 5 minutes
Cook Time: 3½ hours

Festive Bacon & Cheese Dip

2 packages (8 ounces each) cream cheese, cut into cubes
4 cups (16 ounces) shredded Colby-Jack cheese
1 cup half-and-half
2 tablespoons prepared mustard
1 tablespoon minced onion
2 teaspoons Worcestershire sauce
½ teaspoon salt
¼ teaspoon hot pepper sauce
1 pound bacon, crisp-cooked and crumbled

1. Combine cream cheese, Colby-Jack cheese, half-and-half, mustard, onion, Worcestershire sauce, salt and hot pepper sauce in slow cooker.

2. Cover; cook, stirring occasionally, on LOW 1 hour or until cheese melts.

3. Stir in bacon; adjust seasonings. Serve with crusty bread or vegetable dippers.
Makes about 4 cups dip

Parmesan Ranch Snack Mix

Hearty Calico Bean Dip

¾ pound ground beef
½ pound sliced bacon, crisp-cooked and crumbled
1 can (about 16 ounces) baked beans
1 can (about 15 ounces) Great Northern beans, rinsed and drained
1 can (about 15 ounces) kidney beans, rinsed and drained
1 small onion, chopped
½ cup packed brown sugar
½ cup ketchup
1 tablespoon cider vinegar
1 teaspoon prepared yellow mustard
Tortilla chips

1. Brown ground beef in large nonstick skillet over medium-high heat, stirring to break up meat. Drain. Spoon meat into slow cooker.

2. Add bacon, beans, onion, brown sugar, ketchup, vinegar and mustard to slow cooker; mix well.

3. Cover; cook on LOW 4 hours or on HIGH 2 hours. Serve with tortilla chips.

Makes 12 servings

Helpful Hint

Bacon can be easily cooked in a microwave oven. Simply place bacon strips without overlapping in a single layer between several layers of paper towels on a plate. Microwave about 1 minute per slice. Check for doneness three-fourths of the way through the cooking time. Cool bacon before crumbling.

Hearty Calico Bean Dip

Brats in Beer

1½ pounds bratwurst (about 5 or 6 links)
1 can or bottle (12 ounces) beer (not dark)
1 medium onion, thinly sliced
2 tablespoons packed brown sugar
2 tablespoons red wine or cider vinegar
   Spicy brown mustard
   Cocktail rye bread

1. Combine bratwurst, beer, onion, brown sugar and vinegar in slow cooker.

2. Cover; cook on LOW 4 to 5 hours.

3. Remove bratwurst from cooking liquid. Cut into ½-inch-thick slices. For mini open-faced sandwiches, spread mustard on cocktail rye bread. Top with bratwurst slices and onions. *Makes 30 to 36 appetizers*

Tip: Choose a light-tasting beer for cooking brats. Hearty ales might leave the meat tasting slightly bitter.

Prep Time: 5 minutes
Cook Time: 4 to 5 hours

Curried Snack Mix

3 tablespoons butter
2 tablespoons packed light brown sugar
1½ teaspoons hot curry powder
¼ teaspoon salt
¼ teaspoon ground cumin
2 cups rice cereal squares
1 cup walnut halves
1 cup dried cranberries

Melt butter in large skillet. Add brown sugar, curry powder, salt and cumin; mix well. Add cereal, walnuts and cranberries; stir to coat. Transfer mixture to slow cooker. Cover; cook on LOW 3 hours. Cook, uncovered, an additional 30 minutes. Store snack mix in airtight container. *Makes 16 servings*

Brats in Beer

Easy Taco Dip

½ pound ground beef chuck
1 cup frozen corn, thawed
½ cup chopped onion
½ cup salsa
½ cup mild taco sauce
1 can (4 ounces) diced mild green chilies
1 can (4 ounces) sliced ripe olives, drained
1 cup (4 ounces) shredded Mexican cheese blend
Tortilla chips
Sour cream

1. Brown ground beef in large nonstick skillet over medium-high heat, stirring to break up meat. Drain. Spoon into slow cooker.

2. Add corn, onion, salsa, taco sauce, chilies and olives to slow cooker; mix well. Cover; cook on LOW 2 to 3 hours.

3. Just before serving, stir in cheese. Serve with tortilla chips and sour cream.

Makes about 3 cups dip

Tip: To keep this dip hot through your entire party, simply leave it in the slow cooker on LOW or WARM.

Prep Time: 15 minutes
Cook Time: 2 to 4 hours

Easy Taco Dip

Party Mix

3 cups rice cereal squares
2 cups toasted oat cereal rings
2 cups bite-size shredded wheat cereal
1 cup peanuts or pistachio nuts
1 cup thin pretzel sticks
½ cup (1 stick) butter, melted
1 tablespoon Worcestershire sauce
1 teaspoon seasoned salt
½ teaspoon garlic powder
⅛ teaspoon ground red pepper (optional)

1. Combine cereals, nuts and pretzels in slow cooker.

2. Mix butter, Worcestershire sauce, seasoned salt, garlic powder and red pepper in small bowl. Pour over cereal mixture in slow cooker; toss lightly to coat.

3. Cover; cook on LOW 3 hours, stirring well every 30 minutes. Cook, uncovered, 30 minutes. Store cool Party Mix in airtight container. *Makes 10 cups*

Creamy Cheesy Spinach Dip

2 packages (10 ounces each) frozen chopped spinach, thawed
2 cups chopped onions
1 teaspoon salt
½ teaspoon garlic powder
¼ teaspoon black pepper
12 ounces pasteurized processed cheese spread with jalapeño peppers, cubed
Assorted crackers (optional)
Cherry tomatoes with pulp removed (optional)

1. Drain spinach and squeeze dry, reserving ¾ cup liquid. Place spinach, reserved liquid, onions, salt, garlic powder and pepper into 1½-quart slow cooker; stir to blend. Cover; cook on HIGH 1½ hours.

2. Stir in cheese and cook 30 minutes longer or until melted. Serve with crackers or fill cherry tomato shells. *Makes about 4 cups dip*

Tip: To thaw spinach quickly, remove paper wrapper from spinach containers. Microwave at HIGH 3 to 4 minutes or until just thawed.

Party Mix

Honey-Sauced Chicken Wings

  3 pounds chicken wings
  1 teaspoon salt
  ½ teaspoon black pepper
  1 cup honey
  ½ cup soy sauce
  ¼ cup chopped onion
  ¼ cup ketchup
  2 tablespoons vegetable oil
  2 cloves garlic, minced
  ¼ teaspoon red pepper flakes
  Toasted sesame seeds (optional)

1. Rinse chicken and pat dry. Cut off and discard wing tips. Cut each wing at joint to make two sections. Sprinkle wing parts with salt and pepper. Place wings on broiler pan. Broil 4 to 5 inches from heat 20 minutes, turning once or until chicken is brown. Place chicken into slow cooker.

2. For sauce, combine honey, soy sauce, onion, ketchup, oil, garlic and pepper flakes in bowl. Pour over chicken wings.

3. Cover; cook on LOW 4 to 5 hours or on HIGH 2 to 2½ hours. Garnish with sesame seeds, if desired. *Makes about 32 appetizers*

Helpful Hint

To toast sesame seeds, spread seeds in a small skillet. Shake the skillet over medium heat for 2 minutes or until the seeds begin to pop and turn golden brown.

Honey-Sauced Chicken Wings

Hearty Meat Dishes

Italian-Style Pot Roast

2 teaspoons minced garlic
1 teaspoon salt
1 teaspoon dried basil leaves
1 teaspoon dried oregano leaves
¼ teaspoon red pepper flakes
1 boneless beef bottom round rump or chuck shoulder roast (about 2½ to 3 pounds)
1 large onion, quartered and thinly sliced
1½ cups tomato-basil or marinara pasta sauce
2 cans (about 15 ounces each) cannellini or Great Northern beans, rinsed and drained
¼ cup shredded fresh basil or chopped Italian parsley

1. Combine garlic, salt, basil, oregano and pepper flakes in small bowl; rub over roast.

2. Place half of onion slices into slow cooker. Cut roast in half to fit into 4-quart slow cooker. Place one half of roast over onion slices; top with remaining onion slices and other half of roast. Pour pasta sauce over roast. Cover; cook on LOW 8 to 9 hours or until roast is fork tender.

3. Remove roast to cutting board; tent with foil. Let liquid in slow cooker stand 5 minutes to allow fat to rise. Skim off fat.

4. Stir beans into liquid. Cover; cook on HIGH 15 to 30 minutes or until beans are hot. Carve roast across the grain into thin slices. Serve with bean mixture and fresh basil.   *Makes 6 to 8 servings*

Prep Time: 15 minutes
Cook Time: 8 to 9 hours

Italian-Style Pot Roast

Broccoli and Beef Pasta

2 cups broccoli florets *or* 1 package (10 ounces) frozen broccoli, thawed
1 onion, thinly sliced
½ teaspoon dried basil leaves
½ teaspoon dried oregano leaves
½ teaspoon dried thyme leaves
1 can (14½ ounces) Italian-style diced tomatoes, undrained
¾ cup beef broth
1 pound 90% lean ground beef
2 cloves garlic, minced
2 tablespoons tomato paste
2 cups cooked rotini pasta
¾ cup (3 ounces) shredded Cheddar cheese or grated Parmesan cheese

1. Layer broccoli, onion, basil, oregano, thyme, tomatoes with juice and broth in slow cooker. Cover; cook on LOW 2½ hours.

2. Cook and stir beef and garlic in large nonstick skillet over medium-high heat until meat is browned, stirring to break up meat. Drain. Add beef mixture to slow cooker. Cover; cook 2 hours.

3. Stir in tomato paste. Add pasta and cheese. Cover; cook 30 minutes or until cheese melts and mixture is heated through. Sprinkle with additional shredded cheese, if desired. *Makes 4 servings*

Serving Suggestion: Serve with garlic bread.

Broccoli and Beef Pasta

Red Beans and Rice with Ham

1 package (16 ounces) dried red beans, rinsed and sorted
1 pound smoked beef sausage, sliced
1 ham slice (about 8 ounces), cubed
1 small onion, diced
2½ to 3 cups water
1 teaspoon Mexican (adobo) seasoning with pepper
⅛ teaspoon ground red pepper

1. Place beans in large bowl; cover completely with water. Soak 6 to 8 hours or overnight. Drain.

2. Place beans in slow cooker. Add sausage, ham, onion, water (2½ cups for LOW or 3 cups for HIGH), Mexican seasoning and red pepper. Cover; cook on LOW 7 to 8 hours or on HIGH 3 to 4 hours or until beans are tender, stirring every 2 hours, if necessary. Serve over rice. *Makes 6 servings*

Rio Grande Ribs

3 pounds country-style pork ribs, trimmed of all visible fat
1 cup picante sauce
¼ cup beer, non-alcoholic malt beverage or beef broth
1 tablespoon *French's*® Bold n' Spicy Brown Mustard
1 tablespoon *French's*® Worcestershire Sauce
1 teaspoon chili powder
2 tablespoons cornstarch
2 tablespoons water
2 cups *French's*® French Fried Onions, divided

1. Place ribs in slow cooker. Combine picante sauce, beer, mustard, Worcestershire and chili powder in small bowl. Pour mixture over ribs.

2. Cover and cook on LOW setting for 6 hours (or on HIGH for 3 hours) until ribs are tender. Transfer ribs to serving platter; keep warm. Skim fat from sauce.

3. Turn slow cooker to HIGH. Combine cornstarch and water in small bowl; stir into slow cooker. Add *1 cup* French Fried Onions. Cook 15 minutes or until thickened. Spoon sauce over ribs; sprinkle with remaining onions. *Makes 4 to 6 servings*

Prep Time: 10 minutes
Cook Time: about 6 hours

Red Beans and Rice with Ham

Chipotle Taco Filling

2 pounds 85% lean ground beef
2 cups chopped yellow onions
2 cans (about 15 ounces each) pinto beans, rinsed and drained
1 can (14½ ounces) diced tomatoes with peppers and onions, drained
2 chipotle peppers in adobo sauce, mashed
1 tablespoon beef bouillon granules
1 tablespoon sugar
1½ teaspoons ground cumin
Taco shells or flour tortillas

1. Brown meat in large nonstick skillet over medium-high heat, stirring to break up meat. Drain.

2. Combine meat, onions, beans, tomatoes, peppers, bouillon, sugar and cumin in 3½- to 4-quart slow cooker. Cover; cook on LOW 4 hours or on HIGH 2 hours.

3. Serve filling in taco shells. Top with shredded lettuce, salsa, shredded cheese and sour cream, if desired.   *Makes 8 cups filling*

Slow Cooker Taco Shredded Beef

1 boneless beef chuck roast (4 to 4½ pounds)
2 packages (1.0 ounce each) LAWRY'S® Taco Spices & Seasonings
1 medium onion, halved and sliced
2 teaspoons LAWRY'S® Seasoned Salt

Trim and discard all fat from meat; place meat in slow cooker. Sprinkle both packages of Taco Spices & Seasonings over meat and top with onion. Cover and cook on LOW for 8 to 10 hours. Remove beef to platter and shred with fork. Return meat to juices in slow cooker; stir in Seasoned Salt. Serve shredded meat in tacos, burritos, taquitos, flautas, on rolls or over cooked rice.

Makes 8 to 10 servings (or two meals serving 4 to 5)

Prep Time: 10 minutes
Slow Cooker Time: 8 to 10 hours

Chipotle Taco Filling

Beef Stew

5 potatoes, cut into chunks
5 carrots, cut into 1-inch pieces
3 pounds beef for stew (1½-inch cubes)
4 onions, quartered
2 stalks celery, chopped
1 can (about 28 ounces) diced tomatoes, undrained
1½ cups water
1 tablespoon plus 1½ teaspoons salt
1½ teaspoons paprika
1½ teaspoons Worcestershire sauce
¾ teaspoon black pepper
1 clove garlic, minced
1 bay leaf

1. Place potatoes, carrots, beef, onions, celery and tomatoes with juice in 5-quart slow cooker. Blend water with remaining ingredients in medium bowl. Add to slow cooker.

2. Cover; cook on LOW 10 to 12 hours, stir once or twice.

Makes 8 servings

Helpful Hint

The stew meat available in supermarket meat counters is from less tender cuts of beef that are ideal for slow cooking. You can also purchase a chuck roast or boneless beef shoulder roast and cut it yourself into cubes.

Beef Stew

Middle Eastern Lamb & Bean Stew

2 tablespoons olive oil
1 lamb shank (1 to 1½ pounds)
4 cups chicken broth
5 cloves garlic, crushed
8 peppercorns
2 slices bacon, chopped
2 pounds lamb stew meat
½ cup all-purpose flour
½ medium sweet onion, chopped
2 cans (about 15 ounces each) cannellini beans, rinsed and drained
2 carrots, sliced
2 to 3 stalks celery, sliced diagonally into 1-inch slices
¼ cup cornstarch or arrowroot
¼ cup water
   Salt and pepper
   Chopped fresh herbs

1. Heat oil in large skillet over medium-high heat. Brown lamb shank on all sides. Place in 5-quart slow cooker. Add chicken broth, garlic and peppercorns. Cover; cook on HIGH 2 hours.

2. Add bacon to same skillet. Cook until crisp. Remove bacon to paper towels; cool and crumble. Toss stew meat with flour until coated. To same skillet add ½ stew meat; brown on all sides. Place lamb and bacon in slow cooker. Brown remaining stew meat and onion, adding additional oil, if needed. Add lamb mixture, beans, carrots and celery to slow cooker. Cover; cook on LOW 6 hours.

3. Transfer lamb shank to cutting board 30 minutes before serving. Remove meat from bone; return to slow cooker. Discard bone. Let liquid stand 5 minutes to allow fat to rise. Skim off fat. Mix cornstarch and water until smooth. Stir into slow cooker. Cook, uncovered, 30 minutes or until thickened. Season with salt and pepper. Sprinkle with chopped fresh herbs. *Makes 4 to 6 servings*

Middle Eastern Lamb & Bean Stew

Summer Squash Stew

2 pounds bulk Italian turkey sausage
4 cans (14½ ounces each) diced seasoned tomatoes, undrained
5 medium yellow squash, thinly sliced
5 medium zucchini, thinly sliced
1 red onion, finely chopped
2 tablespoons dried Italian seasoning
1 tablespoon dried tomato, basil and garlic salt-free spice seasoning
4 cups (16 ounces) shredded Mexican cheese blend

1. Brown sausage in large nonstick skillet over medium-high heat, stirring to break up meat. Drain. Combine sausage, tomatoes with juice, squash, zucchini, onion and seasonings in 5-quart slow cooker; mix well. Cover; cook on LOW 3 to 4 hours.

2. Sprinkle cheese over stew; cook, uncovered, 15 minutes or until cheese melts.

Makes 6 servings

Autumn Vegetables and Pork Chops

6 pork chops, ¾-inch thick
1 medium-size acorn squash
¾ cup packed brown sugar
3 tablespoons chopped green onion
2 tablespoons butter, melted
2 tablespoons orange juice
1 teaspoon Worcestershire sauce
1 teaspoon grated orange peel
¼ teaspoon ground cinnamon
⅛ teaspoon ground nutmeg
2 cups frozen green peas

Slice acorn squash in half, remove seeds and slice each half into 6 slices, approximately ½ inch thick. Place 6 half slices on bottom of 5-quart slow cooker. Arrange 3 pork chops over squash; repeat layers. Combine remaining ingredients except peas; pour over squash mixture. Cover and cook on LOW 5 to 6 hours or until pork and squash are tender. Remove both from slow cooker; keep warm. Stir in frozen peas. Turn heat setting to HIGH. Cover and cook about 5 minutes or until peas are tender; drain.

Makes 6 servings

Favorite recipe from **National Pork Board**

Summer Squash Stew

Barbara's Pork Chop Dinner

1 tablespoon butter
1 tablespoon olive oil
6 pork loin chops
1 can (10¾ ounces) condensed cream of chicken soup, undiluted
1 can (4 ounces) mushrooms, drained and chopped
¼ cup Dijon mustard
¼ cup chicken broth
2 cloves garlic, minced
½ teaspoon salt
½ teaspoon dried basil leaves
¼ teaspoon black pepper
6 red potatoes, unpeeled, cut into thin slices
1 onion, sliced
Chopped fresh parsley

1. Heat butter and oil in large skillet. Brown pork chops on both sides. Set aside.

2. Combine soup, mushrooms, mustard, chicken broth, garlic, salt, basil and pepper in slow cooker. Add potatoes and onion; stir to coat. Place pork chops on top of potato mixture.

3. Cover; cook on LOW 8 to 10 hours or on HIGH 4 to 5 hours. Sprinkle with parsley just before serving. *Makes 6 servings*

Helpful Hint

Condensed soups are an easy way to create sauces for slow cooker recipes. They provide concentrated flavor and smooth sauces. Use condensed soups undiluted unless directed otherwise in the recipe.

Barbara's Pork Chop Dinner

Beef with Apples & Sweet Potatoes

1 boneless beef chuck shoulder roast (2 pounds)
1 can (40 ounces) sweet potatoes, drained
2 small onions, sliced
2 apples, cored and sliced
½ cup beef broth
2 cloves garlic, minced
1 teaspoon salt
1 teaspoon dried thyme leaves, divided
¾ teaspoon black pepper, divided
1 tablespoon cornstarch
¼ teaspoon ground cinnamon
2 tablespoons cold water

1. Trim fat from beef and cut into 2-inch pieces. Place beef, sweet potatoes, onions, apples, beef broth, garlic, salt, ½ teaspoon thyme and ½ teaspoon pepper in 4-quart slow cooker. Cover; cook on LOW 8 to 9 hours.

2. Transfer beef, sweet potatoes and apples to platter; keep warm. Let liquid stand 5 minutes to allow fat to rise. Skim off fat.

3. Combine cornstarch, remaining ½ teaspoon thyme, ¼ teaspoon pepper, cinnamon and water until smooth; stir into cooking liquid. Cook 15 minutes on HIGH or until juices are thickened. Serve sauce with beef, sweet potatoes and apples.

Makes 6 servings

Prep Time: 20 minutes
Cook Time: 8 to 9 hours

Beef with Apples & Sweet Potatoes

Mushroom-Beef Stew

1 pound beef for stew
1 can (10¾ ounces) condensed cream of mushroom soup, undiluted
2 cans (4 ounces each) sliced mushrooms, drained
1 package (about 1 ounce) dry onion soup mix

Combine all ingredients in slow cooker. Cover; cook on LOW 8 to 10 hours.
Garnish as desired.   *Makes 4 servings*

Serving suggestion: Serve this simple stew over hot seasoned cooked noodles
or rice.

Italian Sausage and Peppers

3 cups (1-inch) bell pepper chunks (preferably a mix of red, yellow
  and green*)
1 small onion, cut into thin wedges
3 cloves garlic, minced
1 pound hot or mild Italian sausage links
1 cup marinara pasta sauce
¼ cup red wine or port wine
1 tablespoon cornstarch
1 tablespoon water
  Hot cooked spaghetti
¼ cup grated Parmesan or Romano cheese

**Look for mixed bell pepper chunks at your supermarket salad bar. Or substitute
3 medium bell peppers (any color or combination) cut into chunks.*

1. Coat slow cooker with cooking spray. Place bell peppers, onion and garlic in
bottom of slow cooker. Arrange sausage over vegetables. Combine pasta sauce and
wine; pour into slow cooker. Cover; cook on LOW 8 to 9 hours or on HIGH 4 to
5 hours or until sausage is no longer pink in center and vegetables are tender.

2. Transfer sausage to serving platter; cover with foil to keep warm. Skim off and
discard fat from liquid in slow cooker. Turn heat to HIGH. Mix cornstarch and water
until smooth; stir into slow cooker. Cook 15 minutes or until sauce is thickened, stirring
once. Serve sauce over spaghetti and sausage; top with cheese.

Makes 4 servings

Mushroom-Beef Stew

Peachy Pork

2 cans (about 15 ounces each) sliced peaches in heavy syrup, undrained
6 to 8 boneless pork blade or top loin chops (about 2 pounds)
1 small onion, thinly sliced
½ cup golden raisins
¼ cup packed light brown sugar
3 tablespoons cider vinegar
2 tablespoons tapioca
1 teaspoon salt
¾ teaspoon ground cinnamon
¼ teaspoon red pepper flakes
2 tablespoons cornstarch
2 tablespoons water

1. Cut peach slices in half. Place peaches with juice, pork chops, onion, raisins, sugar, vinegar, tapioca, salt, cinnamon and pepper flakes into slow cooker. Cover; cook on LOW 7 to 8 hours.

2. Remove pork to warm platter. Skim off fat from peach mixture. Mix cornstarch and water until smooth; stir into peach mixture. Cook on HIGH 15 minutes or until sauce is thickened. Adjust seasonings, if desired.   *Makes 6 to 8 servings*

Prep Time: 15 minutes
Cook Time: 7 to 8 hours

Peachy Pork

Special Sauerbraten

2 cups dry red wine
2 cups red wine vinegar
2 cups water
2 large onions, sliced
2 large carrots, sliced
¼ cup sugar
1 tablespoon dried parsley flakes
2 teaspoons salt
1 teaspoon mustard seeds
6 peppercorns
6 whole cloves
4 juniper berries*
4 bay leaves
1 beef round tip roast (about 5 pounds)
4 tablespoons all-purpose flour, divided
1 teaspoon salt
¼ teaspoon black pepper
2 tablespoons oil
2 tablespoons sugar
⅓ cup gingersnap crumbs

Juniper berries are available in the spice aisle at large supermarkets or from mail order spice purveyors.

1. Stir together wine, vinegar, water, onions, carrots, sugar, parsley, salt, mustard seeds, peppercorns, cloves, juniper berries and bay leaves in medium saucepan over high heat. Bring to a boil. Reduce heat to medium-low and simmer 15 minutes. Cool completely. Place roast in large glass bowl or large resealable plastic food storage bag; pour mixture over roast. Cover or seal bag. Marinate in refrigerator up to 2 days, turning once a day.

2. Remove meat from marinade. Strain marinade; discard vegetables, reserving marinade. Dry meat with paper towel. Mix 2 tablespoons flour, salt and pepper in small bowl; coat all sides of meat. Heat oil in large skillet over medium heat; add meat and brown on all sides. Place meat in 5-quart slow cooker; add 1½ cups strained marinade. Discard remaining marinade. Cover; cook on LOW 8 hours.

3. Combine sugar, remaining 2 tablespoons flour and gingersnap crumbs; add to slow cooker and stir well. Cover; cook on HIGH 30 minutes.

Makes 6 to 8 servings

Special Sauerbraten

Slow-Cooked Korean Beef Short Ribs

4 to 4½ pounds beef short ribs
¼ cup chopped green onions with tops
¼ cup tamari or soy sauce
¼ cup beef broth or water
1 tablespoon brown sugar
2 teaspoons minced fresh ginger
2 teaspoons minced garlic
½ teaspoon black pepper
2 teaspoons dark sesame oil
Hot cooked rice or linguini pasta
2 teaspoons sesame seeds, toasted

1. Place ribs in 5-quart slow cooker. Combine green onions, tamari, broth, brown sugar, ginger, garlic and pepper in medium bowl; mix well and pour over ribs. Cover; cook on LOW 7 to 8 hours or until ribs are fork tender.

2. Remove ribs from cooking liquid. Cool slightly. Trim excess fat. Cut rib meat into bite-size pieces, discarding bones and fat.

3. Let cooking liquid stand 5 minutes to allow fat to rise. Skim off fat.

4. Stir sesame oil into liquid. Return beef to slow cooker. Cover; cook 15 to 30 minutes or until hot.

5. Serve with rice; garnish with sesame seeds.   *Makes 6 servings*

Prep Time: 10 to 15 minutes
Cook Time: 7 to 8 hours

Slow-Cooked Korean Beef Short Ribs

Sweet and Sour Spareribs

4 pounds pork spareribs
2 cups dry sherry or chicken broth
½ cup pineapple, mango or guava juice
⅓ cup chicken broth
2 tablespoons packed light brown sugar
2 tablespoons cider vinegar
2 tablespoons soy sauce
1 clove garlic, minced
½ teaspoon salt
¼ teaspoon black pepper
⅛ teaspoon red pepper flakes
2 tablespoons cornstarch
¼ cup water

1. Preheat oven to 400°F. Place ribs in foil-lined shallow roasting pan. Bake 30 minutes, turning after 15 minutes. Remove from oven. Cut meat into 2-rib portions. Place ribs in 5-quart slow cooker. Add remaining ingredients, except cornstarch and water, to slow cooker.

2. Cover; cook on LOW 6 hours. Transfer ribs to platter; keep warm. Let liquid in slow cooker stand 5 minutes to allow fat to rise. Skim off fat.

3. Blend cornstarch and water until smooth. Stir mixture into slow cooker; mix well. Cook, uncovered, on HIGH 15 minutes or until slightly thickened.

Makes 4 servings

Sweet and Sour Spareribs

Veal Stew with Horseradish

1¼ pounds lean veal, cut into 1-inch cubes
2 medium sweet potatoes, peeled and cut into 1-inch pieces
1 can (14½ ounces) diced tomatoes, undrained
1 package (10 ounces) frozen corn, thawed
1 package (9 ounces) frozen lima beans, thawed
1 large onion, chopped
1 cup vegetable broth
1 tablespoon chili powder
1 tablespoon extra-hot prepared horseradish
1 tablespoon honey

1. Place all ingredients in slow cooker; mix well.

2. Cover; cook on LOW 7 to 8 hours or until veal is tender.   *Makes 6 servings*

Best-Ever Barbecued Ribs

1 teaspoon paprika or smoked paprika
1 teaspoon salt
1 teaspoon dried thyme leaves
¼ teaspoon black pepper
⅛ teaspoon ground red pepper
3 to 3½ pounds well-trimmed pork baby back ribs, cut into 4-rib pieces
¼ cup ketchup
2 tablespoons packed brown sugar
1 tablespoon Worcestershire sauce
1 tablespoon soy sauce

1. Coat 4-quart slow cooker with cooking spray. Combine paprika, salt, thyme and peppers; rub into meaty sides of ribs. Place ribs in slow cooker. Cover; cook on LOW 7 to 8 hours or on HIGH 3 to 3½ hours or until ribs are tender but not falling off the bone.

2. Combine ketchup, brown sugar, Worcestershire sauce and soy sauce; mix well. Remove ribs from slow cooker; discard liquid. Coat ribs with sauce; return to slow cooker. Cook on HIGH 30 minutes or until ribs are glazed.   *Makes 6 servings*

Veal Stew with Horseradish

Hearty Chili Mac

1 pound 90% lean ground beef
1 can (14½ ounces) diced tomatoes, drained
1 cup chopped onion
1 tablespoon chili powder
1 clove garlic, minced
½ teaspoon salt
½ teaspoon ground cumin
½ teaspoon dried oregano leaves
¼ teaspoon red pepper flakes
¼ teaspoon black pepper
2 cups cooked macaroni

1. Brown ground beef in large nonstick skillet over medium-high heat, stirring to separate meat. Drain. Add beef, tomatoes, onion, chili powder, garlic, salt, cumin, oregano, pepper flakes and black pepper to slow cooker; mix well.

2. Cover; cook on LOW 4 hours.

3. Stir in macaroni. Cover; cook 1 hour. *Makes 4 servings*

Helpful Hint

Long, slow cooking maximizes the heat from red pepper flakes. To lessen the heat, add pepper flakes during the last 30 minutes of cooking rather than at the beginning of the cooking process.

Hearty Chili Mac

Classic Cabbage Rolls

   6 cups water
12 large cabbage leaves
   1 pound lean ground lamb
½ cup cooked rice
   1 teaspoon salt
¼ teaspoon dried oregano leaves
¼ teaspoon ground nutmeg
¼ teaspoon black pepper
1½ cups tomato sauce

1. Bring water to a boil in large saucepan. Turn off heat. Soak cabbage leaves in water 5 minutes; remove, drain and cool leaves.

2. Combine lamb, rice, salt, oregano, nutmeg and pepper in large bowl; mix well. Place 2 tablespoonfuls mixture in center of each cabbage leaf; roll firmly. Place cabbage rolls in slow cooker, seam side down. Pour tomato sauce over cabbage rolls.

3. Cover; cook on LOW 8 to 10 hours. *Makes 6 servings*

Irish Stew

   1 cup fat-free reduced-sodium chicken broth
   1 teaspoon dried marjoram leaves
   1 teaspoon dried parsley flakes
¾ teaspoon salt
½ teaspoon garlic powder
¼ teaspoon black pepper
1¼ pounds white potatoes, peeled and cut into 1-inch pieces
   1 pound lean lamb stew meat (1-inch cubes)
   8 ounces frozen cut green beans
   2 small leeks, cut lengthwise into halves then crosswise into slices
1½ cups coarsely chopped carrots

1. Combine broth, marjoram, parsley, salt, garlic powder and pepper in large bowl; mix well. Pour mixture into slow cooker.

2. Layer potatoes, lamb, green beans, leeks and carrots. Cover; cook on LOW 7 to 9 hours or until lamb is tender. *Makes 6 servings*

Classic Cabbage Rolls

Italian-Style Sausage with Rice

1 pound mild Italian sausage links, cut into 1-inch pieces
1 can (about 15 ounces) pinto beans, rinsed and drained
1 cup pasta sauce
1 green bell pepper, cut into strips
1 small onion, halved and sliced
½ teaspoon salt
¼ teaspoon black pepper
Hot cooked rice
Chopped fresh basil (optional)

1. Brown sausage in large nonstick skillet over medium heat. Drain.

2. Place sausage, beans, pasta sauce, bell pepper, onion, salt and black pepper into slow cooker. Cover; cook on LOW 4 to 6 hours.

3. Serve with rice. Garnish with basil, if desired.   *Makes 4 to 5 servings*

Prep Time: 10 to 15 minutes
Cook Time: 4 to 6 hours

Iron Range Pot Roast

1 (3-pound) boneless pork shoulder (Boston Butt) roast
2 teaspoons Italian seasoning
1 teaspoon fennel seed, crushed
1 teaspoon salt
½ teaspoon celery seed
½ teaspoon ground black pepper
2 large potatoes, peeled and cut into ¾-inch slices
4 garlic cloves, peeled and sliced
¾ cup beef broth (or water)

Mix together seasonings and rub over all surfaces of pork roast. Brown roast in a little oil in large skillet over medium-high heat, turning often to brown evenly. Place potatoes and garlic in 3½ to 4-quart slow cooker; pour broth over and top with browned pork roast. Cover and cook on LOW for 8 to 9 hours, until pork is very tender. Slice pork to serve with vegetables and juices.   *Makes 6 to 8 servings*

Favorite recipe from **National Pork Board**

Italian-Style Sausage with Rice

Harvest Ham Supper

6 carrots, cut into 2-inch pieces
3 sweet potatoes, quartered
1½ pounds boneless ham
1 cup maple syrup

1. Place carrots and potatoes in bottom of slow cooker. Place ham on top of vegetables. Pour syrup over ham and vegetables.

2. Cover; cook on LOW 6 to 8 hours or until vegetables are tender.

Makes 6 servings

Dijon Pork Roast with Cranberries

¼ teaspoon allspice
¼ teaspoon salt
¼ teaspoon ground black pepper
1 boneless pork loin roast (2 to 2½ pounds), trimmed of excess fat
2 tablespoons *French's*® Honey Dijon Mustard
2 tablespoons honey
2 teaspoons grated orange peel
1⅓ cups *French's*® French Fried Onions, divided
1 cup dried cranberries

1. Combine allspice, salt and pepper; sprinkle over roast. Place meat in slow cooker. Blend mustard, honey and orange peel; pour over roast. Sprinkle with ⅔ *cup* French Fried Onions and cranberries.

2. Cover and cook on LOW for 4 to 6 hours (or on HIGH for 2 to 3 hours) until meat is fork-tender.

3. Remove pork to serving platter. Skim fat from sauce in slow cooker; transfer sauce to serving bowl. Slice meat and serve with fruit sauce; sprinkle with remaining onions.

Makes 6 servings

Note: Cook times vary depending on type of slow cooker used. Check manufacturer's recommendations for cooking pork roast.

Prep Time: 10 minutes
Cook Time: 6 hours

Harvest Ham Supper

Mexican Meatloaf

2 pounds ground beef
2 cups crushed corn chips
1 cup (4 ounces) shredded Cheddar cheese
⅔ cup salsa
2 eggs, beaten
¼ cup taco seasoning

1. Combine all ingredients in large bowl; mix well.

2. Shape meat mixture into loaf and place in slow cooker. Cover; cook on LOW 8 to 10 hours. *Makes 4 to 6 servings*

Tip: To glaze meatloaf, mix ½ cup ketchup, 2 tablespoons brown sugar and 1 teaspoon dry mustard. Spread over cooked meatloaf. Cover; cook on HIGH 15 minutes.

Beef Stew with Bacon, Onion and Sweet Potatoes

1 pound lean beef stew meat (1-inch chunks)
1 can (about 14 ounces) beef broth
2 medium sweet potatoes, peeled, cut into 2-inch chunks
1 large onion, cut into 1½-inch chunks
2 slices thick-cut bacon, diced
1 teaspoon dried thyme leaves
1 teaspoon salt
¼ teaspoon black pepper
2 tablespoons cornstarch
2 tablespoons water

1. Coat slow cooker with cooking spray. Combine all ingredients except cornstarch and water in slow cooker; mix well. Cover; cook on LOW 7 to 8 hours or on HIGH 4 to 5 hours or until meat and vegetables are tender.

2. With slotted spoon, transfer beef and vegetables to serving bowl; cover with foil to keep warm. Turn slow cooker to HIGH. Mix cornstarch with water until smooth. Stir into juices; cover and cook 15 minutes or until thickened. Spoon sauce over beef and vegetables. *Makes 4 servings*

Mexican Meatloaf

Slow Cooker Brisket of Beef

1 whole well-trimmed beef brisket (about 5 pounds)
2 teaspoons bottled minced garlic
½ teaspoon black pepper
2 large onions, cut into ¼-inch slices and separated into rings
1 bottle (12 ounces) chili sauce
12 ounces beef broth, dark ale or water
2 tablespoons Worcestershire sauce
1 tablespoon packed brown sugar

1. Place brisket, fat side down, in 4- or 5-quart slow cooker. Spread garlic evenly over brisket; sprinkle with pepper. Arrange onions over brisket. Combine chili sauce, broth, Worcestershire sauce and sugar in medium bowl; pour over brisket and onions. Cover; cook on LOW 8 hours.

2. Turn brisket over; stir onions into sauce and spoon over brisket. Cover; cook about 1 hour or until brisket is tender. Transfer brisket to cutting board. Tent with foil; let stand 10 minutes.*

3. Stir juices in slow cooker. Spoon off and discard fat from juices. (Juices may be thinned to desired consistency with water or thickened by simmering, uncovered, in saucepan.) Carve brisket across grain into thin slices. Spoon juices over brisket.

Makes 10 to 12 servings

At this point, brisket may be covered and refrigerated up to one day before serving. To reheat brisket, cut diagonally into thin slices. Place brisket slices and juice in large skillet. Cover and cook over medium-low heat until heated through.

Slow Cooker Brisket of Beef

Slow Cooker Mesquite Beef

1 boneless beef chuck roast (about 4 to 5 pounds)
1 cup LAWRY'S® Mesquite Marinade with Lime Juice, divided
French rolls, flour tortillas or taco shells (optional)

Trim fat from meat. Place meat in large slow cooker. Pour ¾ cup Mesquite Marinade over meat. Cover and cook on LOW for 9 to 10 hours. Remove meat to platter and shred with fork. Return meat to slow cooker with juices; add remaining ¼ cup Mesquite Marinade. Serve shredded beef in warmed French rolls or in warmed flour tortillas or taco shells, if desired.

Makes 8 to 10 servings (or two meals of 4 to 5 servings each)

Meal Idea: Add your favorite frozen stew vegetables during the last hour of cooking for a pot roast/stew meal.

Prep Time: 3 to 4 minutes
Slow Cooker Time: 9 to 10 hours

Cajun Beef Stew

1 tablespoon Cajun or blackened seasoning mix
1 pound beef stew meat (1½-inch chunks)
1 pound red potatoes, cut into 1½-inch chunks
1 medium onion, cut into thin wedges
1½ cups baby carrots
1 can (about 14 ounces) beef broth
3 tablespoons cornstarch
3 tablespoons water
Chopped parsley or thyme (optional)

1. Coat slow cooker with cooking spray. Sprinkle seasoning mix over meat in medium bowl; toss to coat. Place potatoes, onion and carrots in bottom of slow cooker. Place meat over vegetables. Add broth. Cover; cook on LOW 7 to 8 hours or on HIGH 4 to 5 hours or until beef and vegetables are tender.

2. With slotted spoon, transfer beef and vegetables to serving bowl; cover with foil to keep warm. Turn slow cooker to HIGH. Mix cornstarch with water until smooth. Stir into juices; cover and cook on HIGH 15 to 20 minutes or until thickened. Season with salt, if desired. Spoon sauce over beef and vegetables. *Makes 4 servings*

Slow Cooker Mesquite Beef

Cabbage Rolls

    1 large head cabbage, cored
      Salt
    3 pounds ground beef
    1 pound bulk pork sausage
    2 medium onions, chopped
 1½ cups cooked rice
    1 egg
    2 tablespoons prepared horseradish
    2 tablespoons ketchup
    1 package (about 1 ounce) dry onion soup mix
    1 tablespoon salt
    1 teaspoon ground allspice
  ½ teaspoon garlic powder
      Black pepper
      Sauce for Cabbage Rolls (recipe follows)

1. In large stockpot filled halfway with salted water, place cabbage, core side down. Simmer 5 minutes or until outside leaves come off easily. Continue to simmer and pull out rest of leaves. Set leaves aside; reserve cabbage water.

2. Stir together remaining ingredients except Sauce in large mixing bowl. Shape meat mixture into 3-inch balls. Place one meat ball into each cabbage leaf; roll up, fold in edges and secure with toothpick. Repeat with remaining meat mixture and cabbage.

3. Place cabbage rolls in 5-quart slow cooker. Cover; cook on HIGH 3 to 4 hours. Prepare Sauce for Cabbage Rolls. Pour sauce over top of rolls.

Makes about 16 servings

Sauce for Cabbage Rolls

    3 cans (10¾ ounces each) condensed cheese soup, undiluted
    1 can (10¾ ounces) condensed tomato soup, undiluted
 2½ cups reserved cabbage water

Heat all ingredients in medium saucepan over medium heat until hot.

Cabbage Rolls

Fiesta Rice and Sausage

2 pounds spicy Italian sausage, casings removed
2 cloves garlic, minced
2 teaspoons ground cumin
4 onions, chopped
4 green bell peppers, chopped
3 jalapeño peppers, seeded and minced*
4 cups beef broth
2 packages (about 6 ounces each) long grain and wild rice mix

Jalapeño peppers can sting and irritate the skin; wear rubber gloves when handling peppers and do not touch eyes. Wash hands after handling.

1. Brown sausage in large nonstick skillet over medium-high heat, stirring to break up meat. Add garlic and cumin; cook 30 seconds. Add onions, bell peppers and jalapeño peppers. Cook and stir about 10 minutes or until onions are tender. Place mixture in slow cooker.

2. Stir in beef broth and rice.

3. Cover; cook on LOW 4 to 6 hours or on HIGH 2 to 3 hours.

Makes 10 to 12 servings

Helpful Hint

When seeding jalapeño peppers be sure to remove the membranes as well. The heat of chili peppers intensifies during long slow cooking, so it is best to remove the seeds and membranes to better control the heat level.

Fiesta Rice and Sausage

Slow Cooker Steak Fajitas

1 beef flank steak (about 1 pound)
1 medium onion, cut into strips
½ cup medium salsa
2 tablespoons fresh lime juice
2 tablespoons chopped fresh cilantro
2 cloves garlic, minced
1 tablespoon chili powder
1 teaspoon ground cumin
½ teaspoon salt
1 small green bell pepper, cut into strips
1 small red bell pepper, cut into strips
Flour tortillas, warmed
Additional salsa

1. Cut flank steak lengthwise in half, then crosswise into thin strips. Combine onion, ½ cup salsa, lime juice, cilantro, garlic, chili powder, cumin and salt in slow cooker.

2. Cover; cook on LOW 5 to 6 hours. Add bell peppers. Cover; cook on LOW 1 hour.

3. Serve with flour tortillas and additional salsa. *Makes 4 servings*

Prep Time: 20 minutes
Cook Time: 6 to 7 hours

Slow Cooker Steak Fajitas

Slow Cooker Rouladen

12 slices top round beef, pounded thin (¼ inch thick)
Salt and black pepper
Garlic pepper
4 tablespoons Dijon mustard
1½ cups chopped onions
1½ cups chopped dill pickle
Nonstick cooking spray
¼ cup (½ stick) butter
5 tablespoons all-purpose flour
2 cans (about 14 ounces each) beef broth
1 pound baby carrots
4 stalks celery, cut into 1-inch pieces

1. Place 1 slice of beef on cutting board; season with salt, pepper and garlic pepper. Spread with about 1 teaspoon mustard; top with about 2 tablespoons each onion and pickle. Starting at one short side of beef fold about ⅓ of slice over on itself, tuck in long sides, then roll tightly. Secure with toothpick. Repeat with remaining slices of beef, salt, pepper, garlic pepper, onions and pickles.

2. Spray large nonstick skillet with cooking spray. Brown rolled beef slices on all sides in batches over medium-high heat. Remove from skillet.

3. In same skillet, melt butter. Stir in flour. Stir in beef broth. Cook and stir until mixture thickens.

4. Pour half of broth mixture into slow cooker. Add carrots and celery. Top with beef rolls; cover with remaining broth mixture.

5. Cover; cook on LOW 8 to 10 hours or on HIGH 4 to 5 hours until beef and carrots are tender. *Makes 6 to 8 servings*

Slow Cooker Rouladen

Mediterranean Meatball Ratatouille

1 pound bulk mild Italian sausage
1 package (8 ounces) sliced mushrooms
1 small eggplant, diced
1 zucchini, diced
½ cup chopped onion
1 clove garlic, minced
1 teaspoon dried oregano leaves, divided
1 teaspoon salt, divided
½ teaspoon black pepper, divided
2 tomatoes, diced
2 tablespoons tomato paste
2 tablespoons chopped fresh basil
1 teaspoon fresh lemon juice

1. Shape sausage into 1-inch meatballs. Brown meatballs in large nonstick skillet over medium heat. Place half the meatballs in slow cooker. Add half each of mushrooms, eggplant and zucchini. Top with onion, garlic, ½ teaspoon oregano, ½ teaspoon salt and ¼ teaspoon pepper.

2. Add remaining meatballs, mushrooms, eggplant and zucchini, ½ teaspoon oregano, ½ teaspoon salt and ¼ teaspoon pepper. Cover; cook on LOW 6 to 7 hours.

3. Stir in diced tomatoes and tomato paste. Cover; cook on HIGH 15 minutes. Stir in basil and lemon juice; serve.   *Makes 6 (1⅔ cups) servings*

Mediterranean Meatball Ratatouille

Spareribs Simmered in Orange Sauce

4 pounds pork spareribs
2 tablespoons vegetable oil
2 medium onions, cut into ¼-inch slices
1 to 2 tablespoons dried ancho chilies, seeded and finely chopped
½ teaspoon ground cinnamon
¼ teaspoon ground cloves
1 can (about 16 ounces) tomatoes, undrained
2 cloves garlic
½ cup orange juice
⅓ cup dry white wine
⅓ cup packed brown sugar
1 teaspoon shredded orange peel
½ teaspoon salt
1 to 2 tablespoons cider vinegar
Orange wedges (optional)

1. Trim excess fat from ribs. Cut into individual riblets. Heat oil in large skillet over medium heat. Add ribs; cook 10 minutes or until browned on all sides. Remove to plate. Discard all but 2 tablespoons drippings from skillet. Add onions, chilies, cinnamon and cloves. Cook and stir 4 minutes or until onions are softened. Transfer onion mixture to 5-quart slow cooker.

2. Process tomatoes with juice and garlic in food processor or blender until smooth. Combine tomato mixture, orange juice, wine, sugar, orange peel and salt in slow cooker. Add ribs; stir to coat.

3. Cover; cook on LOW 5 hours or until ribs are fork-tender. Remove ribs to plates. Ladle liquid into medium bowl. Let stand 5 minutes. Skim and discard fat. Stir in vinegar; serve sauce over ribs. Garnish with orange wedges, if desired.

Makes 4 to 6 servings

Spareribs Simmered in Orange Sauce

Slow Cooker Pizza Casserole

1½ pounds ground beef
1 pound bulk pork sausage
4 jars (14 ounces each) pizza sauce
2 cups (8 ounces) shredded mozzarella cheese
2 cups grated Parmesan cheese
2 cans (4 ounces each) mushroom stems and pieces, drained
2 packages (3 ounces each) sliced pepperoni
½ cup finely chopped onion
½ cup finely chopped green bell pepper
1 clove garlic, minced
1 pound rotini pasta, cooked and drained

1. Brown beef and sausage in large nonstick skillet over medium-high heat, stirring to break up meat. Drain. Place meat in slow cooker. Add all remaining ingredients except pasta; stir until blended.

2. Cover; cook on LOW 3½ hours or on HIGH 2 hours. Stir in pasta. Cover; cook 30 minutes or until pasta is hot. *Makes 6 servings*

Slow Cooker Pizza Casserole

Mexican-Style Shredded Beef

1 boneless beef chuck shoulder roast (about 3 pounds)
1 tablespoon ground cumin
1 tablespoon ground coriander
1 tablespoon chili powder
1 teaspoon salt
½ teaspoon ground red pepper
1 cup salsa or picante sauce
2 tablespoons water
1 tablespoon cornstarch

1. Cut roast in half. Combine cumin, coriander, chili powder, salt and red pepper in small bowl. Rub over roast. Place ¼ cup salsa in slow cooker; top with one piece roast. Layer ¼ cup salsa, remaining roast and ½ cup salsa in slow cooker. Cover; cook on LOW 8 to 10 hours or until roast is tender.

2. Remove roast from cooking liquid; cool slightly. Trim and discard excess fat from beef. Shred meat with two forks.

3. Let cooking liquid stand 5 minutes to allow fat to rise. Skim off fat. Blend water and cornstarch until smooth. Whisk into liquid in slow cooker. Cook, uncovered, 15 minutes on HIGH until thickened. Return beef to slow cooker. Cover; cook 15 minutes or until hot. Adjust seasonings, if desired. Serve as meat filling for tacos, fajitas or burritos. Leftover beef may be refrigerated up to 3 days or frozen up to 3 months. *Makes 5 cups filling*

Prep Time: 12 minutes
Cook Time: 8 to 10 hours

Mexican-Style Shredded Beef

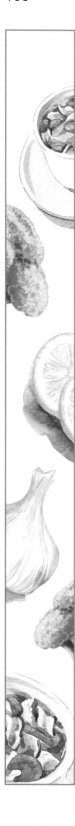

Potluck Poultry

Chicken with Italian Sausage

10 ounces bulk mild or hot Italian sausage
6 boneless skinless chicken thighs
1 can (about 15 ounces) cannellini or Great Northern beans, rinsed and drained
1 can (about 15 ounces) red beans, rinsed and drained
1 cup chicken broth
1 medium onion, chopped
1 teaspoon black pepper
½ teaspoon salt
Chopped fresh parsley

1. Brown sausage in large skillet over medium-high heat, stirring to break up meat. Drain. Spoon sausage into slow cooker.

2. Trim fat from chicken. Place chicken, beans, broth, onion, pepper and salt in slow cooker. Cover; cook on LOW 5 to 6 hours.

3. Adjust seasonings, if desired. Slice each chicken thigh on the diagonal. Serve with sausage and beans. Garnish with parsley, if desired.   *Makes 6 servings*

Prep Time: 15 minutes
Cook Time: 5 to 6 hours

Chicken with Italian Sausage

Chinese Cashew Chicken

1 pound fresh bean sprouts *or* 1 can (16 ounces) bean sprouts, drained
2 cups sliced cooked chicken
1 can (10¾ ounces) condensed cream of mushroom soup, undiluted
1 cup sliced celery
½ cup chopped green onions
1 can (4 ounces) sliced mushrooms, drained
3 tablespoons butter
1 tablespoon soy sauce
1 cup whole cashews
   Hot cooked rice

1. Combine bean sprouts, chicken, soup, celery, onions, mushrooms, butter and soy sauce in slow cooker; mix well.

2. Cover; cook on LOW 4 to 6 hours or on HIGH 2 to 3 hours.

3. Stir in cashews just before serving. Serve with rice.   *Makes 4 servings*

Italian Stew

1 can (about 14 ounces) chicken broth
1 can (14½ ounces) Italian stewed tomatoes with peppers and onions, undrained
1 package (9 ounces) fully cooked spicy chicken sausage, sliced
2 carrots, thinly sliced
2 small zucchini squash, sliced
1 can (about 16 ounces) Great Northern, cannellini or navy beans, rinsed and drained
2 tablespoons chopped fresh basil (optional)

1. Coat slow cooker with cooking spray. Combine all ingredients except beans and basil in slow cooker. Cover; cook on LOW 6 to 7 hours or HIGH 3 to 4 hours, or until vegetables are tender.

2. Turn slow cooker to HIGH; stir in beans. Cover; cook 10 to 15 minutes or until beans are heated through. Ladle into shallow bowls; top with basil, if desired.

Makes 4 servings

Chinese Cashew Chicken

Turkey with Pecan-Cherry Stuffing

1 fresh or frozen boneless turkey breast (about 3 to 4 pounds)
2 cups cooked rice
⅓ cup chopped pecans
⅓ cup dried cherries or cranberries
1 teaspoon poultry seasoning
¼ cup peach, apricot or plum preserves
1 teaspoon Worcestershire sauce

1. Thaw turkey breast, if frozen. Remove and discard skin. Cut slices three-fourths of the way through turkey at 1-inch intervals.

2. Stir together rice, pecans, cherries and poultry seasoning in large bowl. Stuff rice mixture between slices. If needed, skewer turkey lengthwise to hold it together.

3. Place turkey in slow cooker. Cover; cook on LOW 5 to 6 hours or until turkey registers 170°F on meat thermometer inserted into thickest part of breast, not touching stuffing.

4. Stir together preserves and Worcestershire sauce. Spoon over turkey. Cover; let stand for 5 minutes. Remove skewer before serving. *Makes 8 servings*

Serving Suggestion: Serve with asparagus spears, crescent rolls and a spinach salad.

Prep Time: 20 minutes
Cook Time: 5 to 6 hours
Stand Time: 5 minutes

Turkey with Pecan-Cherry Stuffing

Chicken Sausage Pilaf

1 pound chicken or turkey sausages, casings removed
1 cup uncooked rice and pasta mix
4 cups chicken broth
2 ribs celery, diced
¼ cup slivered almonds
Salt and black pepper

1. Brown sausage in large nonstick skillet over medium heat, stirring to break up meat. Drain. Add rice and pasta mix to skillet. Cook 1 minute.

2. Place mixture in slow cooker. Add broth, celery, almonds, salt and pepper to slow cooker; mix well.

3. Cover; cook on LOW 7 to 10 hours or on HIGH 3 to 4 hours or until rice is tender.   *Makes 4 servings*

Arroz con Pollo

6 chicken thighs, skin removed
1 can (14½ ounces) chicken broth
1 can (14½ ounces) stewed tomatoes
1 package (10 ounces) frozen peas
1 package (8 ounces) Spanish-style yellow rice mix
1½ cups *French's*® French Fried Onions, divided

1. Coat slow cooker with vegetable cooking spray. Combine chicken, broth and tomatoes in slow cooker. Cover and cook on LOW setting for 4 to 5 hours (or on HIGH for 2 to 2½ hours) until chicken is fork-tender.

2. Stir in peas and rice mix. Cover and cook on LOW setting for 2 to 3 hours (or on HIGH for 1 to 1½ hours) until rice is cooked and all liquid is absorbed. Stir in ¾ *cup* French Fried Onions. Spoon soup into serving bowls; top with remaining onions.
                                        Makes 6 servings

Note: Cook times vary depending on type of slow cooker used. Check manufacturer's recommendations for cooking chicken and rice.

Prep Time: 10 minutes
Cook Time: 8 hours

Chicken Sausage Pilaf

Easy Parmesan Chicken

8 ounces mushrooms, sliced
1 medium onion, cut in thin wedges
1 tablespoon olive oil
4 boneless skinless chicken breasts
1 jar (26 ounces) pasta sauce
½ teaspoon dried basil leaves
¼ teaspoon dried oregano leaves
1 bay leaf
½ cup (2 ounces) shredded part-skim mozzarella cheese
¼ cup grated Parmesan cheese
  Hot cooked spaghetti

1. Place mushrooms and onion in slow cooker.

2. Heat oil in large skillet over medium-high heat until hot. Lightly brown chicken on both sides. Place chicken in slow cooker. Pour pasta sauce over chicken; add herbs. Cover; cook on LOW 6 to 7 hours or on HIGH 3 to 4 hours or until chicken is tender. Remove and discard bay leaf.

3. Sprinkle chicken with cheeses. Cook, uncovered, on LOW 15 to 30 minutes or until cheeses are melted. Serve over spaghetti. *Makes 4 servings*

Note: Other vegetables, such as sliced zucchini, cubed eggplant or broccoli florets, can be substituted for the mushroom slices.

Prep Time: 10 minutes
Cook Time: 6 to 7 hours

Easy Parmesan Chicken

Mu Shu Turkey

 1 can (16 ounces) plums, drained and pitted
½ cup orange juice
¼ cup finely chopped onion
 1 tablespoon minced fresh ginger
¼ teaspoon ground cinnamon
 1 pound boneless turkey breast, cut into thin strips
 6 (7-inch) flour tortillas
 3 cups coleslaw mix

1. Place plums in blender or food processor. Cover; blend until almost smooth. Combine plums, orange juice, onion, ginger and cinnamon in slow cooker; mix well.

2. Place turkey over plum mixture. Cover; cook on LOW 3 to 4 hours.

3. Remove turkey from slow cooker. Divide evenly among tortillas. Spoon about 2 tablespoons plum sauce over turkey in each tortilla; top with about ½ cup coleslaw mix. Fold bottom edge of tortilla over filling; fold in sides. Roll up to completely enclose filling. Repeat with remaining tortillas. Use remaining plum sauce for dipping.

Makes 6 servings

Sweet Jalapeño Mustard Turkey Thighs

 3 turkey thighs, skin removed
¾ cup honey mustard
½ cup orange juice
 1 tablespoon cider vinegar
 1 teaspoon Worcestershire sauce
 1 to 2 fresh jalapeño peppers,* finely chopped
 1 clove garlic, minced
½ teaspoon grated orange peel

Jalapeño peppers can sting and irritate the skin; wear rubber gloves when handling peppers and do not touch eyes. Wash hands after handling.

Place turkey thighs in single layer in slow cooker. Combine remaining ingredients in large bowl. Pour mixture over turkey thighs. Cover; cook on LOW 5 to 6 hours or until turkey is tender.

Makes 6 servings

Mu Shu Turkey

French Country Slow Cooker Chicken

1 medium onion, chopped
4 carrots, cut into ¼-inch slices
4 ribs celery, cut into slices
6 to 8 boneless skinless chicken breasts (about 1½ to 2 pounds)
1 teaspoon dried tarragon leaves
1 teaspoon dried thyme leaves
  Salt and black pepper
1 can (10¾ ounces) condensed cream of chicken soup, undiluted
1 envelope (about 1 ounce) dry onion soup mix
⅓ cup white wine or apple juice
2 tablespoons cornstarch
  Hot cooked rice

1. Place onion, carrots and celery in slow cooker. Arrange chicken over vegetables. Sprinkle with tarragon, thyme, salt and pepper.

2. Pour soup over chicken. Sprinkle with dry soup mix. Cover; cook on HIGH 3 to 4 hours, stirring once during cooking.

3. Blend wine and cornstarch in small bowl until smooth. Stir into slow cooker. Cook, uncovered, 15 minutes or until sauce thickens. Serve over rice.

Makes 6 to 8 servings

French Country Slow Cooker Chicken

South-of-the-Border Cumin Chicken

1 package (16 ounces) frozen bell pepper stir-fry mixture, thawed
   or* 3 bell peppers, thinly sliced
4 chicken drumsticks
4 chicken thighs
1 can (14½ ounces) stewed tomatoes
1 tablespoon mild green pepper sauce
2 teaspoons sugar
1¾ teaspoons ground cumin, divided
1¼ teaspoons salt
1 teaspoon dried oregano leaves
¼ cup chopped fresh cilantro leaves
1 to 2 medium limes, cut into wedges

*If using fresh bell peppers, add 1 small onion, chopped.

1. Place bell pepper mixture in slow cooker; arrange chicken on top of peppers.

2. Combine tomatoes, pepper sauce, sugar, 1 teaspoon cumin, salt and oregano in large bowl. Pour over chicken mixture. Cover; cook on LOW 8 hours or on HIGH 4 hours or until meat is just beginning to fall off bone.

3. Place chicken in shallow serving bowl. Stir remaining ¾ teaspoon cumin into tomato mixture and pour over chicken. Sprinkle with cilantro and serve with lime wedges. Serve over cooked rice or with toasted corn tortillas, if desired.

Makes 4 servings

Serving suggestion: Serve over cooked rice or with toasted corn tortillas.

South-of-the-Border Cumin Chicken

Turkey and Macaroni

      1 teaspoon vegetable oil
 1½ pounds lean ground turkey
      2 cans (10¾ ounces each) condensed tomato soup, undiluted
      1 can (16 ounces) corn, drained
 ½ cup chopped onion
      1 can (4 ounces) sliced mushrooms, drained
      2 tablespoons ketchup
      1 tablespoon mustard
         Salt and black pepper
      2 cups uncooked macaroni, cooked and drained

1. Heat oil in large nonskillet over medium-high heat; Brown turkey, stirring to separate meat. Transfer turkey to slow cooker.

2. Add soup, corn, onion, mushrooms, ketchup, mustard, salt and pepper to slow cooker; mix well.

3. Cover; cook on LOW 6 to 8 hours or on HIGH 3 to 4 hours. Stir in macaroni. Cover; cook 30 minutes.   *Makes 4 to 6 servings*

Thai-Style Chicken Thighs

      1 teaspoon ground ginger
 ½ teaspoon salt
 ¼ teaspoon ground red pepper
      6 bone-in chicken thighs (about 2¼ pounds), skinned
      1 medium onion, chopped
      3 cloves garlic, minced
 ⅓ cup canned coconut milk
 ¼ cup peanut butter
      2 tablespoons soy sauce
      1 tablespoon cornstarch
      2 tablespoons water
      3 cups hot cooked couscous or yellow rice
 ¼ cup chopped cilantro

continued on page 126

Turkey and Macaroni

Thai-Style Chicken Thighs, continued

1. Coat slow cooker with cooking spray. Combine ginger, salt and pepper; sprinkle over meaty sides of chicken. Place onion and garlic in slow cooker; top with chicken. Whisk together coconut milk, peanut butter and soy sauce; pour over chicken. Cover; cook on LOW 6 to 7 hours or HIGH 3 to 4 hours, or until chicken is tender.

2. With slotted spoon, transfer chicken to serving bowl; cover with foil to keep warm. Turn slow cooker to HIGH. Combine cornstarch with water until smooth. Stir into juices; cover and cook 15 minutes or until sauce is slightly thickened. Spoon sauce over chicken. Serve chicken over couscous; top with cilantro. Garnish with lime wedges, if desired. *Makes 6 servings*

Chicken and Stuffing

½ cup all-purpose flour
¾ teaspoon seasoned salt
¾ teaspoon black pepper
4 to 6 boneless skinless chicken breasts (about 1 to 1½ pounds)
¼ cup (½ stick) butter
2 cans (10¾ ounces each) condensed cream of mushroom soup, undiluted
1 package (12 ounces) seasoned stuffing mix, plus ingredients to prepare mix

1. Combine flour, seasoned salt and pepper in large resealable plastic food storage bag; add chicken. Seal bag; shake to coat with flour mixture.

2. Melt butter in large skillet over medium-low heat. Brown chicken on both sides. Place in slow cooker; pour soup over chicken.

3. Prepare stuffing according to package directions, decreasing liquid by half. Arrange stuffing over chicken. Cover; cook on HIGH 3 to 4 hours or until chicken is tender. *Makes 4 to 6 servings*

Chicken and Stuffing

Coconut Chicken Curry

    1 tablespoon vegetable oil
    4 boneless skinless chicken breasts
    3 medium potatoes, peeled and chopped
    1 medium onion, sliced
    1 can (14 ounces) coconut milk
    1 cup chicken broth
 1½ teaspoons curry powder
    1 teaspoon hot pepper sauce
  ½ teaspoon salt
  ½ teaspoon black pepper
    1 package (10 ounces) frozen peas, thawed

1. Heat oil in large skillet over medium-high heat. Brown chicken on both sides. Place potatoes and onion in slow cooker. Top with chicken.

2. Combine coconut milk, broth, curry powder, pepper sauce, salt and pepper in medium bowl. Pour over chicken. Cover; cook on LOW 6 to 8 hours.

3. About 30 minutes before serving, add peas to slow cooker. Serve over hot cooked rice; if desired. *Makes 4 servings*

Chutney Curried Chicken with Yogurt Sauce

    1 container (6 to 8 ounces) plain low-fat yogurt
    2 teaspoons curry powder
    1 teaspoon garlic salt
 ⅛ teaspoon ground red pepper
    4 bone-in chicken breast halves, skin removed (2 to 2¼ pounds)
    1 small onion, sliced
 ⅓ cup mango chutney (chop large pieces of mango, if necessary)
    1 tablespoon lime juice
    2 cloves garlic, minced
    2 tablespoons cornstarch
    2 tablespoons water
    3 cups hot cooked lo mein noodles or linguini
     Chopped cilantro, chopped peanuts or toasted coconut for garnish

continued on page 130

Coconut Chicken Curry

Chutney Curried Chicken with Yogurt Sauce, continued

1. Coat slow cooker with cooking spray. Place yogurt in paper-towel-lined strainer over a bowl. Drain in refrigerator until serving time.

2. Sprinkle curry powder, garlic salt and pepper over chicken. Place onion in slow cooker; top with chicken. Combine chutney, lime juice and garlic; spoon over chicken. Cover; cook on LOW 5 to 6 hours or HIGH 2½ to 3 hours, or until chicken is tender.

3. With slotted spoon, transfer chicken to serving platter; cover with foil to keep warm. Turn slow cooker to HIGH. Combine cornstarch with water until smooth. Stir into juices; cook, covered, 15 minutes or until thickened. Spoon sauce over chicken; serve over noodles. Top with thickened yogurt and garnish as desired.

Makes 4 servings

Cheesy Slow Cooker Chicken

> **6 boneless skinless chicken breasts (about 1½ pounds)**
> **Salt**
> **Black pepper**
> **Garlic powder**
> **2 cans (10¾ ounces each) condensed cream of chicken soup, undiluted**
> **1 can (10¾ ounces) condensed Cheddar cheese soup, undiluted**
> **Chopped fresh parsley (optional)**

1. Place 3 chicken breasts in slow cooker. Sprinkle with salt, pepper and garlic powder. Repeat with remaining 3 breasts and seasonings.

2. Combine soups in medium bowl; pour over chicken. Cover; cook on LOW 6 to 8 hours or until chicken is tender. Garnish with parsley, if desired.

Makes 6 servings

Serving suggestion: Serve this cheesy chicken over pasta, rice or mashed potatoes.

Cheesy Slow Cooker Chicken

Turkey Mushroom Stew

1 pound turkey cutlets, cut into 4×1-inch strips
1 small onion, thinly sliced
2 tablespoons minced green onion
8 ounces mushrooms, sliced
2 to 3 tablespoons all-purpose flour
1 cup half-and-half or milk
1 teaspoon salt
1 teaspoon dried tarragon leaves
Black pepper
½ cup frozen peas
½ cup sour cream
Puff pastry shells

1. Layer turkey, onion and mushrooms in slow cooker. Cover; cook on LOW 4 hours.

2. Remove turkey and vegetables to serving bowl. Blend flour, half-and-half, salt, tarragon and pepper until smooth. Stir into slow cooker. Return cooked vegetables and turkey to slow cooker. Stir in peas. Cover; cook on HIGH 30 to 45 minutes or until sauce has thickened and peas are heated through.

3. Stir in sour cream just before serving. Serve in puff pastry shells.

Makes 4 servings

Helpful Hint

Avoid cooking large quantities of frozen vegetables in the slow cooker. When added at the beginning of the cooking process, they can delay the food from reaching a safe temperature (140°F). Frozen vegetables are best used thawed or added in small quantities near the end of the cooking time.

Turkey Mushroom Stew

Continental Chicken

    1 package (2¼ ounces) dried beef, cut into pieces
    4 boneless skinless chicken breasts (about 1 pound)
    4 slices lean bacon
    1 can (10¾ ounces) condensed cream of mushroom soup, undiluted
¼ cup all-purpose flour
¼ cup reduced-fat sour cream
    Hot cooked noodles

1. Spray inside of slow cooker with nonstick cooking spray. Place dried beef in bottom of slow cooker. Wrap each piece of chicken with one bacon slice. Place wrapped chicken on top of dried beef.

2. Combine soup and flour in medium bowl; mix until smooth. Pour over chicken.

3. Cover; cook on LOW 7 to 9 hours or on HIGH 3 to 4 hours. Add sour cream during last 30 minutes of cooking. Serve over noodles. *Makes 4 servings*

Chicken Teriyaki

    1 pound boneless skinless chicken tenders
    1 can (6 ounces) pineapple juice
¼ cup soy sauce
    1 tablespoon sugar
    1 tablespoon minced fresh ginger
    1 tablespoon minced garlic
    1 tablespoon vegetable oil
    1 tablespoon molasses
24 cherry tomatoes (optional)
    2 cups hot cooked rice

Combine all ingredients except rice in slow cooker. Cover; cook on LOW 2 hours or until chicken is tender. Serve chicken and sauce over rice. *Makes 4 servings*

Continental Chicken

Chicken Parisienne

6 boneless skinless chicken breasts (about 1½ pounds), cubed
½ teaspoon salt
½ teaspoon black pepper
½ teaspoon paprika
1 can (10¾ ounces) condensed cream of mushroom or cream of
    chicken soup, undiluted
2 cans (4 ounces each) sliced mushrooms, drained
½ cup dry white wine
1 cup sour cream
6 cups hot cooked egg noodles

1. Place chicken in slow cooker. Sprinkle with salt, pepper and paprika. Add soup, mushrooms and wine to slow cooker; mix well.

2. Cover; cook on HIGH 2 to 3 hours.

3. Add sour cream during last 30 minutes of cooking. Serve over noodles. Garnish as desired. *Makes 6 servings*

Creamy Chicken

3 boneless skinless chicken breasts *or* 6 boneless skinless chicken
    thighs
2 cans (10¾ ounces each) condensed cream of chicken soup,
    undiluted
1 can (14½ ounces) chicken broth
1 can (4 ounces) sliced mushrooms, drained
½ medium onion, diced
    Salt
    Black pepper

Place all ingredients except salt and pepper in slow cooker. Cover; cook on LOW 6 to 8 hours. Season to taste with salt and pepper. *Makes 3 servings*

Note: If desired, you may add cubed processed cheese spread before serving.

Chicken Parisienne

Chicken Stew

4 to 5 cups chopped cooked chicken (about 5 boneless skinless chicken breasts)
1 can (about 28 ounces) whole tomatoes, cut up, undrained
2 large potatoes, peeled and cut into 1-inch pieces
8 ounces fresh okra, sliced
1 large onion, chopped
1 can (14 ounces) cream-style corn
½ cup ketchup
½ cup barbecue sauce

1. Combine chicken, tomatoes with juice, potatoes, okra and onion in slow cooker. Cover; cook on LOW 6 to 8 hours or until potatoes are tender.

2. Add corn, ketchup and barbecue sauce. Cover; cook on HIGH 30 minutes.

Makes 6 servings

Southwestern-Style Chicken

1 package (about 1¼ ounces) taco seasoning mix
¼ cup all-purpose flour
6 to 8 boneless skinless chicken thighs or 4 boneless skinless breasts, cut in half
2 tablespoons vegetable oil
1 large onion, cut into 1-inch pieces
2 green bell peppers, cut into 1-inch pieces
1 can (14½ ounces) diced tomatoes with jalapeños, undrained
Salt and pepper

1. Reserve 1 teaspoon taco seasoning. Combine flour and remaining seasoning in plastic food storage bag. Add chicken, 1 to 2 pieces at a time; shake to coat.

2. Heat oil in large skillet over medium-high heat; brown chicken. Transfer chicken to slow cooker; sprinkle with reserved 1 teaspoon seasoning.

3. In same skillet, add onion to skillet; cook and stir onion until translucent. Place onion, bell peppers and tomatoes with juice in slow cooker. Cover; cook on LOW 6 to 7 hours or until chicken is tender. Season with salt and pepper to taste.

Makes 4 to 6 servings

Chicken Stew

Thai Turkey & Noodles

1 package (about 1½ pounds) turkey tenderloins, cut into ¾-inch pieces
1 red bell pepper, cut into short, thin strips
1¼ cups reduced-sodium chicken broth, divided
¼ cup reduced-sodium soy sauce
3 cloves garlic, minced
¾ teaspoon red pepper flakes
¼ teaspoon salt
2 tablespoons cornstarch
3 green onions, cut into ½-inch pieces
⅓ cup creamy or chunky peanut butter (not natural-style)
12 ounces hot cooked vermicelli pasta
¾ cup peanuts or cashews, chopped
¾ cup cilantro sprigs, chopped

1. Place turkey, bell pepper, 1 cup broth, soy sauce, garlic, pepper flakes and salt in slow cooker. Cover; cook on LOW 3 to 4 hours.

2. Blend cornstarch and remaining ¼ cup broth until smooth. Stir green onions, peanut butter and cornstarch mixture into slow cooker. Cover; cook on HIGH 30 minutes or until sauce is thickened. Stir well.

3. Serve over vermicelli. Sprinkle with peanuts and cilantro.   *Makes 6 servings*

Variation: Substitute ramen noodles for vermicelli. Discard the flavor packet from ramen soup mix and drop the noodles into boiling water. Cook the noodles 2 to 3 minutes or until just tender. Drain and serve hot.

Thai Turkey & Noodles

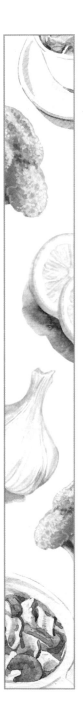

Sweet Chicken Curry

1 pound boneless skinless chicken breasts, cut into 1-inch pieces
1 large green or red bell pepper, cut into 1-inch pieces
1 large onion, sliced
1 large tomato, seeded and chopped
½ cup prepared mango chutney
¼ cup water
2 tablespoons cornstarch
1½ teaspoons curry powder
Hot cooked rice

1. Place chicken, bell pepper and onion in slow cooker. Top with tomato.

2. Mix chutney, water, cornstarch and curry powder in small bowl. Pour over chicken.

3. Cover; cook on LOW 3½ to 4½ hours or until chicken is tender. Serve over rice.

Makes 4 servings

Nice 'n' Easy Italian Chicken

4 boneless skinless chicken breasts (about 1 pound)
8 ounces mushrooms, sliced
1 medium green bell pepper, chopped (optional)
1 medium zucchini, diced
1 medium onion, chopped
1 jar (26 ounces) pasta sauce

Combine all ingredients in slow cooker. Cover; cook on LOW 6 to 8 hours or until chicken is tender.

Makes 4 servings

Serving suggestion: Serve over the hot cooked pasta.

Sweet Chicken Curry

Coq au Vin

2 cups frozen pearl onions, thawed
4 slices thick-cut bacon, crisp-cooked and crumbled
1 cup sliced button mushrooms
1 clove garlic, minced
1 teaspoon dried thyme leaves
⅛ teaspoon black pepper
6 boneless skinless chicken breasts (about 2 pounds)
½ cup dry red wine
¾ cup reduced-sodium chicken broth
¼ cup tomato paste
3 tablespoons all-purpose flour
Hot cooked egg noodles (optional)

1. Layer onions, bacon, mushrooms, garlic, thyme, pepper, chicken, wine and broth in slow cooker.

2. Cover; cook on LOW 6 to 8 hours.

3. Remove chicken and vegetables; cover and keep warm. Ladle ½ cup cooking liquid into small bowl; cool slightly. Mix reserved liquid, tomato paste and flour until smooth; stir into slow cooker. Cook; uncovered, on HIGH 15 minutes or until thickened. Serve over hot noodles, if desired.   *Makes 6 servings*

Helpful Hint

When using wine in recipes, avoid cooking wine. Wine flavors intensify with long cooking so use a good inexpensive wine that you would find drinkable. If you don't finish a bottle of wine, save the leftovers for cooking. Store it refrigerated in small tightly sealed jars and use it within a week.

Coq au Vin

Southwest Turkey Tenderloin Stew

1½ **pounds turkey tenderloins, cut into ¾-inch pieces**
  1 **tablespoon chili powder**
  1 **teaspoon ground cumin**
¼ **teaspoon salt**
  1 **can (about 15 ounces) chili beans in spicy sauce, undrained**
  1 **can (14½ ounces) chili-style stewed tomatoes, undrained**
¾ **cup prepared salsa or picante sauce**
  1 **red bell pepper, cut into ¾-inch pieces**
  1 **green bell pepper, cut into ¾-inch pieces**
¾ **cup chopped red or yellow onion**
  3 **cloves garlic, minced**
    Fresh cilantro (optional)

1. Place turkey in slow cooker. Sprinkle with chili powder, cumin and salt; toss to coat.

2. Add beans, tomatoes with juice, salsa, bell peppers, onion and garlic; mix well. Cover; cook on LOW 5 to 6 hours.

3. Adjust seasonings. Ladle into bowls. Garnish with cilantro, if desired.

Makes 6 servings

Helpful Hint

To tame the spiciness of this recipe, you can substitute chili beans in mild sauce for the spicy version. Be sure to chose a mild salsa.

Southwest Turkey Tenderloin Stew

Moroccan Chicken Tagine

3 pounds chicken pieces, skin removed
2 cups chicken broth
1 can (14½ ounces) diced tomatoes, undrained
2 onions, chopped
1 cup dried apricots, chopped
4 cloves garlic, minced
2 teaspoons ground cumin
1 teaspoon ground cinnamon
1 teaspoon ground ginger
½ teaspoon ground coriander
½ teaspoon ground red pepper
6 sprigs fresh cilantro
1 tablespoon cornstarch
1 tablespoon water
1 can (about 15 ounces) chick-peas, drained and rinsed
2 tablespoons chopped fresh cilantro
¼ cup slivered almonds, toasted
  Hot cooked couscous or rice

1. Place chicken in slow cooker. Combine broth, tomatoes with juice, onions, apricots, garlic, cumin, cinnamon, ginger, coriander, red pepper and cilantro in medium bowl; pour over chicken.

2. Cover; cook on LOW 4 to 5 hours or until chicken is tender. Transfer chicken to serving platter; cover to keep warm.

3. Combine cornstarch and water in small bowl until smooth. Stir cornstarch mixture and chick-peas into slow cooker. Cover; cook on HIGH 15 minutes or until sauce is thickened. Pour sauce over chicken. Sprinkle with cilantro and toasted almonds and serve with couscous.   *Makes 4 to 6 servings*

Tip: To toast almonds, heat small nonstick skillet over medium-high heat. Add almonds; cook and stir about 3 minutes or until golden brown. Remove from pan at once. Let cool before adding to other ingredients.

Moroccan Chicken Tagine

Tuscan Pasta

1 pound boneless skinless chicken breasts, cut into 1-inch pieces
2 cans (14½ ounces each) Italian-style stewed tomatoes
1 can (about 15 ounces) red kidney beans, rinsed and drained
1 can (about 15 ounces) tomato sauce
1 cup water
1 jar (4 ounces) sliced mushrooms, drained
1 medium green bell pepper, chopped
½ cup chopped onion
½ cup chopped celery
4 cloves garlic, minced
1 teaspoon Italian seasoning
6 ounces uncooked thin spaghetti, broken in half

1. Place all ingredients except spaghetti in slow cooker.

2. Cover; cook on LOW 4 hours or until vegetables are tender.

3. Stir in spaghetti. Cook on HIGH 10 minutes; stir. Cover; cook 30 minutes or until spaghetti is tender.   *Makes 8 servings*

Mile-High Enchilada Pie

8 (6-inch) corn tortillas
1 jar (12 ounces) prepared salsa
1 can (about 15 ounces) kidney beans, rinsed and drained
1 cup shredded cooked chicken
1 cup shredded Monterey Jack cheese with jalapeño peppers

Prepare foil handles for slow cooker (see page 15); place in slow cooker. Place 1 tortilla on bottom of slow cooker. Top with small amount of salsa, beans, chicken and cheese. Continue layering using remaining ingredients, ending with tortilla and cheese. Cover; cook on LOW 6 to 8 hours or on HIGH 3 to 4 hours. Lift out with foil handles. Garnish with fresh cilantro and slice of red pepper, if desired.

Makes 4 to 6 servings

Tuscan Pasta

Chicken Pilaf

2 pounds chopped cooked chicken
2 cans (8 ounces each) tomato sauce
2½ cups water
1⅓ cups uncooked long-grain converted rice
1 cup chopped onion
1 cup chopped celery
1 cup chopped green bell pepper
⅔ cup sliced black olives
¼ cup sliced almonds
¼ cup (½ stick) butter or margarine
2 cloves garlic, minced
2½ teaspoons salt
½ teaspoon ground allspice
½ teaspoon ground turmeric
¼ teaspoon curry powder
¼ teaspoon black pepper

1. Combine all ingredients in slow cooker; stir well.

2. Cover; cook on LOW 6 to 8 hours or on HIGH 3 to 4 hours.

Makes 10 servings

Helpful Hint

Rice has a tendency to become mushy when cooked for many hours in a slow cooker. For the best results, choose uncooked converted long-grain rice and begin checking for doneness the last 30 minutes of the cooking time.

Chicken Pilaf

Chicken Vesuvio

      3 tablespoons all-purpose flour
1½ teaspoons dried oregano leaves
      1 teaspoon salt
    ½ teaspoon black pepper
      1 frying chicken, cut up, or 3 pounds bone-in chicken pieces
      2 tablespoons olive oil
      4 small baking potatoes, cut into 8 wedges each
      2 small onions, cut into thin wedges
      4 cloves garlic, minced
    ¼ cup chicken broth
    ¼ cup dry white wine
    ¼ cup chopped parsley
      Lemon wedges (optional)

1. Coat slow cooker with cooking spray. Combine flour, oregano, salt and pepper in resealable plastic food storage bag. Wash chicken; pat dry with paper towels. Trim off and discard any excess fat. Add chicken, several pieces at a time, to bag and shake to coat lightly with flour mixture. Heat oil in large skillet over medium heat until hot. Add chicken; cook 10 to 12 minutes or until browned on all sides.

2. Place potatoes, onion and garlic in slow cooker. Add broth and wine. Transfer chicken to slow cooker; drizzle pan juices from skillet evenly over chicken. Cover; cook on LOW 6 to 7 hours or on HIGH 3 to 3½ hours, or until chicken and potatoes are tender. Transfer chicken and vegetables to serving plates; top with juices from slow cooker. Sprinkle with parsley. Serve with lemon wedges, if desired.

Makes 4 to 6 servings

Chicken Stew with Herb Dumplings

2 cans (about 14 ounces each) chicken broth, divided
2 cups sliced carrots
1 cup chopped onion
1 large green bell pepper, sliced
½ cup sliced celery
⅔ cup all-purpose flour
1 pound boneless skinless chicken breasts, cut into 1-inch pieces
1 large unpeeled potato, cut into 1-inch pieces
6 ounces mushrooms, halved
¾ cup frozen peas
1 teaspoon dried basil leaves
¾ teaspoon dried rosemary leaves
¼ teaspoon dried tarragon leaves
¾ to 1 teaspoon salt
¼ teaspoon black pepper
¼ cup whipping cream

Herb Dumplings
1 cup biscuit baking mix
¼ teaspoon dried basil leaves
¼ teaspoon dried rosemary leaves
⅛ teaspoon dried tarragon leaves
⅓ cup milk

1. Reserve 1 cup chicken broth. Combine carrots, onion, bell pepper, celery and remaining chicken broth in slow cooker. Cover; cook on LOW 2 hours.

2. Stir remaining 1 cup broth into flour until smooth. Stir into slow cooker. Add chicken, potato, mushrooms, peas, 1 teaspoon basil, ¾ teaspoon rosemary and ¼ teaspoon tarragon to slow cooker. Cover; cook 4 hours or until vegetables are tender and chicken is tender. Stir in salt, black pepper and cream.

3. Combine baking mix, ¼ teaspoon basil, ¼ teaspoon rosemary and ¼ teaspoon tarragon in small bowl. Stir in milk to form soft dough. Spoon dumpling mixture on top of stew in 4 large spoonfuls. Cook, uncovered, 30 minutes. Cover; cook 30 to 45 minutes or until dumplings are firm and toothpick inserted in center comes out clean. Serve in shallow bowls. *Makes 4 servings*

Super-Easy Sandwiches

Easy Homemade Barbecue Sandwiches

Water
1 boneless pork shoulder (butt) roast (3 to 4 pounds)
Salt
Black pepper
1 bottle (16 ounces) barbecue sauce
Hamburger buns or sandwich rolls

1. Cover bottom of slow cooker with water. Place roast in slow cooker; season with salt and pepper.

2. Cover; cook on LOW 8 to 10 hours.

3. Remove roast from slow cooker; let stand 15 minutes. Discard liquid remaining in slow cooker. Shred cooked roast using 2 forks. Return meat to slow cooker. Add barbecue sauce; mix well. Cover and cook on HIGH 30 minutes. Serve mixture on toasted buns. *Makes 8 to 10 servings*

Serving suggestion: Serve with your favorite coleslaw recipe.

Easy Homemade Barbecue Sandwich

Hot & Juicy Reuben Sandwiches

1 mild-cure corned beef (about 1½ pounds)
2 cups sauerkraut, drained
½ cup beef broth
1 small onion, sliced
1 clove garlic, minced
¼ teaspoon caraway seeds
4 to 6 peppercorns
8 slices pumpernickel or rye bread
4 slices Swiss cheese
Mustard

1. Trim excess fat from corned beef. Place meat in slow cooker. Add sauerkraut, broth, onion, garlic, caraway seeds and peppercorns.

2. Cover; cook on LOW 7 to 9 hours.

3. Remove beef from slow cooker. Cut across the grain into ¼-inch-thick slices. Divide evenly on 4 slices bread. Top each slice with ½ cup drained sauerkraut mixture and one slice cheese. Spread mustard on remaining 4 bread slices. Close sandwiches. *Makes 4 servings*

Note: This two-fisted stack of corned beef, sauerkraut and melted Swiss cheese makes a glorious sandwich you'll serve often using slow-cooked corned beef.

Prep Time: 25 minutes
Cook Time: 7 to 9 hours

Hot & Juicy Reuben Sandwich

Best Beef Brisket Sandwich Ever

1 beef brisket (about 3 pounds)
2 cups apple cider, divided
1 head garlic, cloves separated, crushed and peeled
2 tablespoons whole peppercorns
⅓ cup chopped fresh thyme *or* 2 tablespoons dried thyme leaves
1 tablespoon mustard seeds
1 tablespoon Cajun seasoning
1 teaspoon ground cumin
1 teaspoon celery seeds
1 teaspoon ground allspice
2 to 4 whole cloves
1 bottle (12 ounces) dark beer
10 to 12 sourdough sandwich rolls, halved (optional)

1. Place brisket, ½ cup cider, garlic, peppercorns, thyme, mustard seeds, Cajun seasoning, cumin, celery seeds, allspice and cloves in large resealable plastic food storage bag. Seal bag; marinate in refrigerator overnight.

2. Place brisket and marinade in slow cooker. Add remaining 1½ cups apple cider and beer.

3. Cover; cook on LOW 10 hours or until brisket is tender. Strain sauce; drizzle over meat. Slice brisket and place on rolls, if desired.   *Makes 10 to 12 servings*

Serving suggestion: For extra-special flavor, serve these sandwiches with mustard spread or horseradish sauce.

Best Beef Brisket Sandwich Ever

Barbecued Beef Sandwiches

3 pounds boneless beef chuck shoulder roast
2 cups ketchup
1 medium onion, chopped
¼ cup cider vinegar
¼ cup dark molasses
2 tablespoons Worcestershire sauce
2 cloves garlic, minced
½ teaspoon salt
½ teaspoon dry mustard
½ teaspoon black pepper
¼ teaspoon garlic powder
¼ teaspoon red pepper flakes
  Sesame seed buns, split

1. Cut roast in half; place in slow cooker. Combine ketchup, onion, vinegar, molasses, Worcestershire sauce, garlic, salt, mustard, black pepper, garlic powder and pepper flakes in large bowl. Pour sauce mixture over roast. Cover; cook on LOW 8 to 10 hours or on HIGH 4 to 5 hours.

2. Remove roast from sauce; cool slightly. Trim and discard excess fat from beef. Shred meat using two forks.

3. Let sauce stand 5 minutes to allow fat to rise. Skim off fat.

4. Return shredded meat to slow cooker. Stir meat to evenly coat with sauce. Adjust seasonings. Cover; cook 15 to 30 minutes or until hot.

5. Spoon filling into sandwich buns and top with additional sauce, if desired.

Makes 12 servings

Prep Time: 20 to 25 minutes
Cook Time: 9 to 10 hours

Barbecued Beef Sandwich

Slow-Cooked Kielbasa in a Bun

1 pound kielbasa, cut into 4 (4- to 5-inch) pieces
1 large onion, thinly sliced
1 large green bell pepper, cut into strips
¼ teaspoon salt
¼ teaspoon dried thyme leaves
¼ teaspoon black pepper
½ cup chicken broth
4 hoagie rolls, split

1. Brown kielbasa in nonstick skillet over medium-high heat 3 to 4 minutes. Place kielbasa in slow cooker. Add onion, bell pepper, salt, thyme and pepper. Stir in chicken broth.

2. Cover; cook on LOW 7 to 8 hours.

3. Place kielbasa in rolls. Top with onion and bell pepper. Serve with favorite condiments.   *Makes 4 servings*

Tip: For zesty flavor, top sandwiches with pickled peppers and a dollop of mustard.

Prep Time: 10 minutes
Cook Time: 7 to 8 hours

Easy Beef Sandwiches

1 large onion, sliced
1 boneless beef bottom round roast (about 3 to 5 pounds)
1 cup water
1 package (1 ounce) au jus gravy mix
6 to 8 French bread rolls, split

Place onion slices in bottom of slow cooker; top with roast. Combine water and au jus mix in small bowl; pour over roast. Cover and cook on LOW 7 to 9 hours or until beef is tender. Transfer beef to cutting board. Using two forks, shred beef; return beef to slow cooker. Serve beef on rolls with beef juices on the side for dipping.
Makes 6 to 8 servings

Serving suggestion: Add slices of provolone cheese to these sandwiches.

Slow-Cooked Kielbasa in a Bun

Italian Beef

1 beef rump roast (3 to 5 pounds)
1 can (14 ounces) beef broth
2 cups mild giardiniera
8 Italian bread rolls

1. Place rump roast in slow cooker; add beef broth and giardiniera.

2. Cover; cook on LOW 10 hours.

3. Transfer beef to cutting board. Shred beef using two forks; return beef to slow cooker and heat briefly. Serve beef with sauce on crusty Italian rolls.

Makes 8 servings

Tex-Mex Beef Wraps

1 tablespoon chili powder
2 teaspoons ground cumin
1 teaspoon salt
¼ teaspoon ground red pepper
1 boneless beef chuck pot roast (2½ to 3 pounds), cut into 4 pieces
1 medium onion, chopped
3 cloves garlic, minced
1 cup salsa, divided
12 (6- to 7-inch) flour or corn tortillas, warmed
1 cup (4 ounces) shredded Cheddar or Monterey Jack cheese
1 cup chopped tomato
¼ cup chopped cilantro
1 ripe avocado, diced

1. Coat slow cooker with cooking spray. Blend chili powder, cumin, salt and red pepper. Rub meat all over with spice mixture. Place onion and garlic in bottom of slow cooker; top with meat. Spoon ½ cup salsa over meat. Cover; cook on LOW 8 to 9 hours or on HIGH 3½ to 4½ hours or until meat is very tender.

2. Remove meat to cutting board; use 2 forks to shred meat. Skim off and discard fat from juices in slow cooker; return meat to slow cooker and mix well. Adjust seasonings. Place meat on warm tortillas; top with cheese, tomato, cilantro and avocado. Fold to enclose filling. Serve with remaining salsa. *Makes 6 servings*

Italian Beef

BBQ Pork Sandwiches

4 pounds boneless pork loin roast, fat trimmed
1 can (14½ ounces) beef broth
⅓ cup *French's*® Worcestershire Sauce
⅓ cup *Frank's*® *RedHot*® Original Cayenne Pepper Sauce

Sauce
½ cup ketchup
½ cup molasses
¼ cup *French's*® Classic Yellow® Mustard
¼ cup *French's*® Worcestershire Sauce
2 tablespoons *Frank's*® *RedHot*® Original Cayenne Pepper Sauce

1. Place roast on bottom of slow cooker. Combine broth, ⅓ *cup each* Worcestershire and **Frank's RedHot** Sauce. Pour over roast. Cover and cook on HIGH 5 hours* or until roast is tender.

2. Meanwhile, combine ingredients for sauce in large bowl; set aside.

3. Transfer roast to large cutting board. Discard liquid. Coarsely chop roast. Stir into reserved sauce. Spoon pork mixture on large rolls. Serve with deli potato salad, if desired.   *Makes 8 to 10 servings*

*Or cook 10 hours on LOW.

Tip: Make additional sauce and serve on the side. Great also with barbecued ribs and chops!

Prep Time: 10 minutes
Cook Time: 5 hours

BBQ Pork Sandwich

Suzie's Sloppy Joes

    3 pounds 90% lean ground beef
    1 cup chopped onion
    3 cloves garlic, minced
1¼ cups ketchup
    1 cup chopped red bell pepper
    5 tablespoons Worcestershire sauce
    4 tablespoons brown sugar
    3 tablespoons prepared mustard
    3 tablespoons vinegar
    2 teaspoons chili powder
    Toasted hamburger buns

1. Brown ground beef, onion and garlic in large nonstick skillet over medium-high heat in two batches, stirring to break up meat. Drain.

2. Combine ketchup, bell pepper, Worcestershire sauce, brown sugar, mustard, vinegar and chili powder in slow cooker. Stir in beef mixture.

3. Cover; cook on LOW 6 to 8 hours. Spoon into hamburger buns.

Makes 8 servings

Helpful Hint

To drain cooked ground meat, place it in a colander. Stir the meat briefly or shake the colander. You can also transfer the meat to the slow cooker using a slotted spoon, which will allow the fat to drain off.

Suzie's Sloppy Joes

Meatball Grinders

1 can (15 ounces) diced tomatoes, drained and juices reserved
1 can (8 ounces) no-salt-added tomato sauce
¼ cup chopped onion
2 tablespoons tomato paste
1 teaspoon dried Italian seasoning
1 pound ground chicken
½ cup fresh whole wheat or white bread crumbs (1 slice bread)
1 egg white, lightly beaten
3 tablespoons finely chopped fresh parsley
2 cloves garlic, minced
¼ teaspoon salt
⅛ teaspoon black pepper
   Nonstick cooking spray
4 small hard rolls, split
2 tablespoons grated Parmesan cheese

1. Combine diced tomatoes, ½ cup reserved juice, tomato sauce, onion, tomato paste and Italian seasoning in slow cooker. Cover; cook on LOW 3 to 4 hours or until onions are soft.

2. Halfway through cooking time, prepare meatballs. Combine chicken, bread crumbs, egg white, parsley, garlic, salt and pepper in medium bowl. With wet hands, form mixture into 12 to 16 meatballs. Spray medium nonstick skillet with cooking spray; heat over medium heat until hot. Add meatballs; cook about 8 to 10 minutes or until well browned on all sides. Remove meatballs to slow cooker; cook on LOW 1 to 2 hours or until meatballs are no longer pink in centers.

3. Place 3 to 4 meatballs in each roll. Spoon sauce over meatballs. Sprinkle with cheese.   *Makes 4 servings*

Meatball Grinder

Shredded Beef Fajitas

1 beef flank steak (about 1½ pounds)
1 can (14½ ounces) diced tomatoes with jalapeños, undrained
1 cup chopped onion
1 medium green bell pepper, cut into ½-inch pieces
2 cloves garlic, minced *or* ¼ teaspoon garlic powder
1 package (1½ ounces) fajita seasoning mix
12 (8-inch) flour tortillas
    Toppings: sour cream, guacamole, shredded Cheddar cheese, salsa (optional)

1. Cut flank steak into 6 portions; place in slow cooker. Combine tomatoes with juice, onion, bell pepper, garlic and seasoning mix in medium bowl. Add tomatoes. Cover; cook on LOW 8 to 10 hours or on HIGH 4 to 5 hours or until beef is tender.

2. Remove beef from slow cooker; shred. Return beef to slow cooker and stir.

3. To serve fajitas, place meat mixture evenly into flour tortillas. Add toppings as desired; roll up tortillas.   *Makes 12 servings*

Easy Beefy Sandwiches

1 boneless beef rump roast (2 to 4 pounds)
1 package (1 ounce) Italian salad dressing mix
1 package (1 ounce) dry onion soup mix
2 cubes beef bouillon
2 tablespoons prepared yellow mustard
    Salt
    Onion powder
    Garlic powder
    Black pepper
1 cup water
6 to 8 crusty rolls, split
    Provolone or mozzarella cheese slices

Place roast, salad dressing mix, soup mix, bouillon cubes and mustard in slow cooker. Season to taste with salt, garlic powder, onion powder and pepper. Add water. Cover; cook on LOW 8 to 10 hours or until beef is tender. Serve beef on rolls with cheese slices.   *Makes 6 to 8 servings*

Shredded Beef Fajita

Hot Beef Sandwiches

1 chuck beef roast (3 to 4 pounds), cut into chunks
1 small jar (6 ounces) sliced dill pickles, undrained
1 medium onion, diced
1 teaspoon mustard seeds
4 cloves garlic, minced
1 can (14 ounces) crushed tomatoes with Italian seasoning
   Hamburger buns

1. Place beef in slow cooker. Pour pickles with juice over beef. Add onion, mustard seeds, garlic and tomatoes. Cover; cook on LOW 8 to 10 hours.

2. Remove beef from slow cooker. Shred beef with two forks. Return beef to slow cooker; mix well. Serve beef mixture on buns. *Makes 6 to 8 servings*

Serving suggestion: Serve sandwiches with lettuce, sliced tomatoes, sliced red onion or slaw mix.

BBQ Beef Sandwiches

1 boneless beef chuck roast (about 3 pounds)
¼ cup ketchup
2 tablespoons brown sugar
2 tablespoons red wine vinegar
1 tablespoon Dijon mustard
1 tablespoon Worcestershire sauce
1 clove garlic, crushed
¼ teaspoon salt
¼ teaspoon liquid smoke
⅛ teaspoon black pepper
10 to 12 French rolls or sandwich buns

1. Place beef in slow cooker. Combine remaining ingredients except rolls in medium bowl; pour over meat.

2. Cover; cook on LOW 8 to 9 hours.

3. Remove beef from slow cooker; shred with 2 forks. Combine beef with 1 cup sauce from slow cooker. Evenly distribute meat and sauce mixture among warmed rolls. *Makes 10 to 12 servings*

Hot Beef Sandwich

Easy Family Burritos

1 boneless beef chuck shoulder roast (2 to 3 pounds)
1 jar (24 ounces) *or* **2 jars (16 ounces each) salsa**
**   Flour tortillas**

1. Place roast in slow cooker; top with salsa. Cover; cook on LOW 8 to 10 hours.

2. Remove beef from slow cooker. Shred meat with 2 forks. Return to slow cooker. Cover; cook 1 to 2 hours or until heated through.

3. Serve shredded meat wrapped in warm tortillas.   *Makes 8 servings*

Serving suggestions: Serve these burritos with toppings of your choice, such as shredded cheese, sour cream, chopped lettuce, chopped tomato, chopped onion or guacamole.

Italian-Style Shredded Beef

1 (2½-pound) boneless eye of round beef roast
1 medium onion, thinly sliced
1 (6-ounce) can Italian flavored tomato paste
6 teaspoons HERB-OX® beef flavored bouillon
½ cup water
12 Kaiser rolls
12 (1-ounce) slices Provolone cheese

Place roast in a 3½-quart slow cooker. Add onion and remaining ingredients. Cover and cook on HIGH for 5 to 6 hours or until meat is tender. Remove roast from cooker. Using two forks, shred meat. Return meat to cooker; stirring to coat with sauce. Evenly divide meat among Kaiser rolls. Top with cheese and serve.   *Makes 12 servings*

Prep Time: 10 minutes
Total Time: 6 hours, 10 minutes

Easy Family Burritos

Sloppy Sloppy Joes

4 pounds ground beef
1 cup chopped onion
1 cup chopped green bell pepper
1 can (about 28 ounces) tomato sauce
2 cans (10¾ ounces each) condensed tomato soup, undiluted
1 cup packed brown sugar
¼ cup ketchup
3 tablespoons Worcestershire sauce
1 tablespoon dry mustard
1 tablespoon prepared mustard
1½ teaspoons chili powder
1 teaspoon garlic powder
Toasted hamburger buns

1. Brown meat in large skillet over medium-high heat, stirring to break up meat. Drain. Add onion and bell pepper; cook and stir 5 to 6 minutes over medium heat or until onion is translucent.

2. Transfer meat mixture to 4- or 5-quart slow cooker. Add remaining ingredients except buns; stir until well blended.

3. Cover; cook on LOW 4 to 6 hours. Serve on buns.   *Makes 20 to 25 servings*

Helpful Hint

One unique difference in slow cooker recipes is that little liquid is needed. If you're new to slow cooking, you'll be surprised how thick this mixture is before cooking. Slow cooking produces steam that can't escape from the covered container; instead it condenses to form liquid that returns to the food.

Sloppy Sloppy Joe

Piping-Hot Soups

Simmering Hot & Sour Soup

   2 cans (about 14 ounces each) chicken broth
   1 cup chopped cooked chicken or pork
   4 ounces fresh shiitake mushroom caps, thinly sliced
½ cup sliced bamboo shoots, cut into thin strips
   3 tablespoons rice vinegar or rice wine vinegar
   2 tablespoons soy sauce
1½ teaspoons Chinese chili sauce or paste *or* 1 teaspoon hot chili oil
   4 ounces firm tofu, well drained and cut into ½-inch pieces
   2 teaspoons dark sesame oil
   2 tablespoons cornstarch
   2 tablespoons cold water
      Chopped cilantro or sliced green onions

1. Combine chicken broth, chicken, mushrooms, bamboo shoots, vinegar, soy sauce and chili sauce in slow cooker. Cover; cook on LOW 3 to 4 hours.

2. Stir in tofu and sesame oil. Blend cornstarch and water until smooth. Stir into slow cooker. Cover; cook on HIGH 15 minutes or until soup is thickened.

3. Serve hot; garnish with cilantro.   *Makes 4 servings*

Prep Time: 10 to 15 minutes
Cook Time: 3 to 4 hours

Simmering Hot & Sour Soup

Italian Beef and Barley Soup

1 boneless beef top sirloin steak (about 1½ pounds)
1 tablespoon vegetable oil
4 medium carrots or parsnips, cut into ¼-inch slices
1 cup chopped onion
1 teaspoon dried thyme leaves
½ teaspoon dried rosemary
¼ teaspoon black pepper
⅓ cup pearl barley
2 cans (about 14 ounces each) beef broth
1 can (14½ ounces) diced tomatoes with Italian seasoning, undrained

1. Cut beef into 1-inch pieces. Heat oil over medium-high heat in large skillet. Brown beef on all sides; set aside.

2. Place carrots and onion in slow cooker; sprinkle with thyme, rosemary and pepper. Top with barley and meat. Pour broth and tomatoes with juice over meat.

3. Cover; cook on LOW 8 to 10 hours. *Makes 6 servings*

Prep Time: 20 minutes
Cook Time: 8 to 10 hours

Helpful Hint

Choose pearl barley rather than quick-cooking barley, which will become mushy during long cooking.

Italian Beef and Barley Soup

Nancy's Chicken Noodle Soup

1 can (48 ounces) chicken broth
2 boneless skinless chicken breasts, cut into bite-size pieces
4 cups water
⅔ cup diced onion
⅔ cup diced celery
⅔ cup diced carrots
⅔ cup sliced mushrooms
½ cup frozen peas
4 chicken bouillon cubes
2 tablespoons margarine
1 tablespoon parsley flakes
1 teaspoon salt
1 teaspoon ground cumin
1 teaspoon dried marjoram leaves
1 teaspoon black pepper
2 cups cooked egg noodles

1. Combine all ingredients except noodles in 5-quart slow cooker.

2. Cover; cook on LOW 5 to 7 hours or on HIGH 3 to 4 hours. Add noodles 30 minutes before serving. *Makes 4 servings*

Nancy's Chicken Noodle Soup

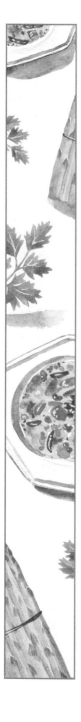

Clam Chowder

5 cans (10¾ ounces each) condensed reduced-fat cream of potato soup, undiluted
2 cans (12 ounces each) evaporated skimmed milk
2 cans (10 ounces each) whole baby clams, rinsed and drained
1 can (about 15 ounces) cream-style corn
2 cans (4 ounces each) tiny shrimp, rinsed and drained
¾ cup crisp-cooked and crumbled bacon (about ½ pound)
   Lemon pepper to taste
   Oyster crackers

Combine all ingredients except crackers in 4-quart slow cooker. Cover; cook on LOW 3 to 4 hours, stirring occasionally. Serve with oyster crackers.   *Makes 10 servings*

Beef, Barley & Onion Soup

2 pounds beef stew meat, (½-inch cubes)
3 large carrots, cut into ½-inch-thick slices
2 large ribs celery, cut into ½-inch-thick slices
4 cans (14½ ounces each) beef broth
½ teaspoon dried oregano leaves
½ teaspoon salt
¼ teaspoon ground black pepper
½ cup barley
2 cups *French's*® French Fried Onions, divided

1. Combine beef, carrots, celery, broth and seasonings in slow cooker. Cover; cook on LOW for 7 hours (or on HIGH for 3½ hours) until meat and vegetables are tender.

2. Stir in barley. Cover and cook on LOW for 1 hour (or on HIGH for ½ hour) until barley is tender. Stir in *1 cup* French Fried Onions. Spoon soup into serving bowls; sprinkle with remaining onions.   *Makes 8 servings*

Note: Cook times vary depending on type of slow cooker used. Check manufacturer's recommendations for cooking beef and barley.

Prep Time: 20 minutes
Cook Time: 8 hours

Clam Chowder

No-Chop Black Bean Soup

3 cans (about 15 ounces each) black beans, rinsed and drained
1 package (12 ounces) frozen diced green bell peppers, thawed
2 cups frozen chopped onion, thawed
2 cans (about 14 ounces each) chicken broth
1 can (14½ ounces) diced tomatoes with pepper, celery and onion, undrained
1 teaspoon bottled minced garlic
1½ teaspoons ground cumin, divided
2 tablespoons olive oil
¾ teaspoon salt

1. Combine beans, bell peppers, onions, broth, tomatoes with juice, garlic and 1 teaspoon cumin in slow cooker.

2. Cover; cook on LOW 8 to 10 hours or on HIGH 4 to 5 hours.

3. Stir in oil, salt and remaining ½ teaspoon cumin just before serving.

Makes 8 servings

Butternut Squash-Apple Soup

3 packages (12 ounces each) frozen cooked winter squash, thawed and drained *or* about 4½ cups mashed cooked butternut squash
2 cans (14½ ounces each) chicken broth
1 medium Golden Delicious apple, peeled, cored and chopped
2 tablespoons minced onion
1 tablespoon packed light brown sugar
1 teaspoon minced fresh sage *or* ½ teaspoon ground sage
¼ teaspoon ground ginger
½ cup whipping cream or half-and-half

1. Combine squash, broth, apple, onion, brown sugar, sage and ginger in slow cooker.

2. Cover; cook on LOW about 6 hours or on HIGH about 3 hours.

3. Purée soup in food processor or blender. Stir in cream just before serving.

Makes 6 to 8 servings

Tip: For thicker soup, use only 3 cups chicken broth.

No-Chop Black Bean Soup

Beef Fajita Soup

1 pound beef stew meat
1 can (about 15 ounces) pinto beans, rinsed and drained
1 can (about 15 ounces) black beans, rinsed and drained
1 can (14½ ounces) diced tomatoes with roasted garlic, undrained
1 can (about 14 ounces) beef broth
1 small green bell pepper, thinly sliced
1 small red bell pepper, thinly sliced
1 small onion, thinly sliced
1½ cups water
2 teaspoons ground cumin
1 teaspoon seasoned salt
1 teaspoon black pepper
Toppings: sour cream, shredded Monterey Jack or Cheddar cheese, chopped olives

1. Combine beef, beans, tomatoes with juice, broth, bell peppers, onion, water, cumin, salt and black pepper in slow cooker.

2. Cover; cook on LOW 8 hours.

3. Serve with desired toppings.

Makes 8 servings

Helpful Hint

Diced tomatoes with seasonings are a great time saver when assembling ingredients for a slow cooker dish. Look for varieties with Italian seasoning, roasted garlic, mushroom and garlic, and mild green chilies.

Beef Fajita Soup

Creamy Turkey Soup

2 cans (10¾ ounces each) condensed cream of chicken soup, undiluted
2 cups chopped cooked turkey breast
1 package (8 ounces) sliced mushrooms
1 medium yellow onion, chopped
1 teaspoon rubbed sage *or* ½ teaspoon dried poultry seasoning
1 cup frozen peas, thawed
½ cup milk
1 jar (about 4 ounces) diced pimiento

1. Combine soup, turkey, mushrooms, onion and sage in slow cooker.

2. Cover; cook on LOW 8 hours or on HIGH 4 hours.

3. Stir in peas, milk and pimiento. Cover; cook on HIGH 15 minutes or until heated through.   *Makes 5 to 6 servings*

Classic French Onion Soup

¼ cup (½ stick) butter
3 large yellow onions, sliced
1 cup dry white wine
3 cans (14½ ounces each) beef or chicken broth
1 teaspoon Worcestershire sauce
½ teaspoon salt
½ teaspoon dried thyme leaves
4 slices French bread, toasted
1 cup (4 ounces) shredded Swiss cheese
Fresh thyme for garnish

1. Melt butter in large skillet over medium-high heat. Add onions; cook and stir 15 minutes or until onions are soft and lightly browned. Stir in wine.

2. Combine onion mixture, broth, Worcestershire sauce, salt and thyme in slow cooker. Cover; cook on LOW 4 to 4½ hours.

3. Ladle soup into 4 bowls; top with bread slice and cheese. Garnish with fresh thyme, if desired.   *Makes 4 servings*

Creamy Turkey Soup

Vegetable Medley Soup

   3 cans (about 14 ounces each) chicken broth
   3 sweet potatoes, peeled and chopped
   3 zucchini, chopped
   2 cups broccoli florets
   2 white potatoes, peeled and shredded
   1 onion, chopped
   1 rib celery, finely chopped
¼ cup (½ stick) butter, melted
   1 teaspoon black pepper
   2 cups half-and-half or milk
   1 tablespoon salt
   1 teaspoon ground cumin

1. Combine chicken broth, sweet potatoes, zucchini, broccoli, white potatoes, onion, celery, butter and pepper in slow cooker.

2. Cover; cook on LOW 8 to 10 hours or on HIGH 4 to 5 hours.

3. Add half-and-half, salt and cumin. Cover; cook 30 minutes to 1 hour or until heated through.   *Makes 12 servings*

Double Thick Baked Potato-Cheese Soup

   2 pounds baking potatoes, peeled and cut into ½-inch cubes
   2 cans (10½ ounces each) condensed cream of mushroom soup
1½ cups finely chopped green onions, divided
¼ teaspoon garlic powder
⅛ teaspoon ground red pepper
1½ cups (6 ounces) shredded sharp Cheddar cheese
   1 cup (8 ounces) sour cream
   1 cup milk
   Black pepper

1. Combine potatoes, soup, 1 cup green onions, garlic powder and red pepper in slow cooker. Cover; cook on LOW 8 hours or on HIGH 4 hours.

2. Add cheese, sour cream and milk; stir until cheese has completely melted. Cover; cook on HIGH 10 minutes. Season to taste with black pepper. Garnish with remaining green onions.   *Makes 7 servings*

Vegetable Medley Soup

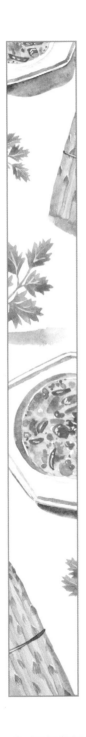

Potato & Spinach Soup with Gouda

9 medium Yukon Gold potatoes, peeled and cubed (about 6 cups)
2 cans (14 ounces each) chicken broth
½ cup water
1 small red onion, finely chopped
5 ounces baby spinach leaves
½ teaspoon salt
¼ teaspoon ground red pepper
¼ teaspoon black pepper
2½ cups shredded smoked Gouda cheese, divided
1 can (12 ounces) evaporated milk
1 tablespoon olive oil
4 cloves garlic, cut into thin slices
5 to 7 sprigs parsley, finely chopped

1. Combine potatoes, chicken broth, water, onion, spinach, salt, red and black pepper in 4-quart slow cooker.

2. Cover; cook on LOW 10 hours or until potatoes are tender.

3. Slightly mash potatoes in slow cooker; add 2 cups Gouda and evaporated milk. Cover; cook on HIGH 15 to 20 minutes or until cheese is melted.

4. Heat oil in small skillet over low heat. Cook and stir garlic until golden brown; set aside. Pour soup into bowls. Sprinkle 2 to 3 teaspoons remaining Gouda cheese in each bowl. Add spoonful of garlic to center of each bowl; sprinkle with parsley.

Makes 8 to 10 servings

Potato & Spinach Soup with Gouda

Red Bean Soup with Andouille Sausage

2 tablespoons unsalted butter
1 large sweet onion, diced
3 stalks celery, diced
2 large cloves garlic, chopped
8 cups chicken broth
1 ham hock
1½ cups dried red kidney beans, soaked in cold water 1 hour, drained and rinsed
1 bay leaf
2 parsnips, diced
1 sweet potato, diced
1 pound andouille smoked sausage or other smoked pork sausage, cut into ½-inch pieces
Salt and black pepper

1. Melt butter in large saucepan over medium heat. Add onion, celery and garlic. Cook and stir 5 minutes. Place in 5- or 6-quart slow cooker. Add broth, ham hock, kidney beans and bay leaf. Cover; cook on HIGH 2 hours.

2. Remove ham hock; discard. Add parsnips and sweet potato. Cover; cook on HIGH 2 hours.

3. Add sausage. Cover; cook an additional 30 minutes or until heated through. Remove and discard bay leaf. Season with salt and pepper.

Makes 6 to 8 servings

Note: Use a 5- or 6-quart slow cooker for this recipe. If you're using a smaller slow cooker, make only half of the recipe.

Red Bean Soup with Andouille Sausage

Chicken and Vegetable Chowder

1 pound boneless skinless chicken breasts, cut into 1-inch pieces
1 can (about 14 ounces) reduced-sodium chicken broth
1 can (10¾ ounces) condensed cream of potato soup
1 package (10 ounces) frozen broccoli florets, thawed
1 cup sliced carrots
1 jar (4½ ounces) sliced mushrooms, drained
½ cup chopped onion
½ cup corn
2 cloves garlic, minced
½ teaspoon dried thyme leaves
⅓ cup half-and-half

1. Combine chicken, broth, soup, broccoli, carrots, mushrooms, onion, corn, garlic and thyme in slow cooker; mix well.

2. Cover; cook on LOW 5 to 6 hours.

3. Stir in half-and-half. Cover; cook on HIGH 15 minutes or until heated through.

Makes 6 servings

Variation: Add ½ cup (2 ounces) shredded Swiss or Cheddar cheese just before serving, stirring over LOW heat until melted.

Helpful Hint

Always add fresh dairy products to the slow cooker during the last 15 to 30 minutes of cooking.

Chicken and Vegetable Chowder

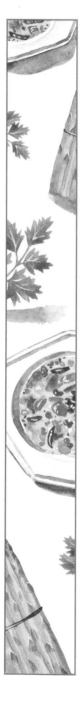

Pasta Fagioli Soup

2 cans (about 14 ounces each) reduced-sodium beef broth
1 can (about 15 ounces) Great Northern beans, rinsed and drained
1 can (14½ ounces) diced tomatoes, undrained
2 medium zucchini, quartered lengthwise and sliced
1 tablespoon olive oil
1½ teaspoons minced garlic
½ teaspoon dried basil leaves
½ teaspoon dried oregano leaves
½ cup uncooked tubetti, ditali or small shell pasta
½ cup garlic seasoned croutons
½ cup grated Asiago or Romano cheese
3 tablespoons chopped fresh basil or Italian parsley (optional)

1. Combine broth, beans, tomatoes with juice, zucchini, oil, garlic, basil and oregano in slow cooker; mix well. Cover; cook on LOW 3 to 4 hours.

2. Stir in pasta. Cover; cook on LOW 1 hour or until pasta is tender.

3. Serve soup with croutons and cheese. Garnish with fresh basil, if desired.

Makes 5 to 6 servings

Prep Time: 12 minutes
Cook Time: 4 to 5 hours

Helpful Hint

Only small pasta varieties like tubetti, ditali or small shell-shaped pasta should be used in this recipe. The low heat of a slow cooker won't allow larger pasta to completely cook.

Pasta Fagioli Soup

Farmhouse Ham and Vegetable Chowder

> **2 cans (10¾ ounces each) condensed cream of celery soup,
>   undiluted**
> **2 cups diced cooked ham**
> **1 package (10 ounces) frozen corn, thawed**
> **1 large baking potato, cut into ½-inch pieces**
> **1 medium red bell pepper, diced**
> **½ teaspoon dried thyme leaves**
> **2 cups small broccoli florets**
> **½ cup milk**

1. Combine soup, ham, corn, potato, bell pepper and thyme in slow cooker; mix well.

2. Cover; cook on LOW 6 to 8 hours or on HIGH 3 to 4 hours.

3. Stir in broccoli and milk. Cover; cook on HIGH 15 to 30 minutes or until broccoli is crisp-tender.   *Makes 6 servings*

Easy Italian Vegetable Soup

> **1 can (14½ ounces) diced tomatoes, undrained**
> **1 can (10½ ounces) condensed beef broth**
> **1 package (8 ounces) sliced mushrooms**
> **1 medium yellow onion, chopped**
> **1 medium zucchini, thinly sliced**
> **1 medium green bell pepper, chopped**
> **⅓ cup dry red wine or beef broth**
> **1½ tablespoons dried basil leaves**
> **2½ teaspoons sugar**
> **1 tablespoon olive oil**
> **½ teaspoon salt**
> **1 cup (4 ounces) shredded Mozzarella cheese (optional)**

1. Combine tomatoes, broth, mushrooms, onion, zucchini, bell pepper, wine, basil and sugar in slow cooker.

2. Cover; cook on LOW 8 hours or on HIGH 4 hours.

3. Stir oil and salt into soup. Garnish with cheese, if desired.

Makes 5 to 6 servings

Farmhouse Ham and Vegetable Chowder

Hamburger Soup

1 pound 90% lean ground beef
1 cup sliced celery
1 cup thinly sliced carrots
1 package (1 ounce) dry onion soup mix
1 package (1 ounce) Italian salad dressing mix
¼ teaspoon seasoned salt
¼ teaspoon black pepper
3 cups boiling water
1 can (14½ ounces) diced tomatoes, undrained
1 can (8 ounces) tomato sauce
1 tablespoon soy sauce
2 cups cooked macaroni
¼ cup grated Parmesan cheese
2 tablespoons chopped fresh parsley

1. Brown beef in large skillet over medium-high heat, stirring to break up meat. Drain. Place celery and carrots in slow cooker. Top with beef, soup mix, salad dressing mix, seasoned salt and pepper. Add water, tomatoes with juice, tomato sauce and soy sauce.

2. Cover; cook on LOW 6 to 8 hours.

3. Stir in macaroni and Parmesan cheese. Cover; cook on HIGH 15 to 30 minutes or until heated through. Sprinkle with parsley just before serving.

Makes 6 to 8 servings

Hamburger Soup

Potato-Crab Chowder

1 package (10 ounces) frozen corn, thawed
1 cup frozen hash brown potatoes, thawed
¾ cup finely chopped carrots
1 teaspoon dried thyme leaves
¾ teaspoon garlic-pepper
3 cups fat-free reduced-sodium chicken broth
½ cup water
1 cup evaporated milk
3 tablespoons cornstarch
1 can (6 ounces) crabmeat, drained
½ cup sliced green onions

1. Place corn, potatoes and carrots in slow cooker. Sprinkle with thyme and garlic-pepper. Add broth and water.

2. Cover; cook on LOW 4 to 5 hours.

3. Blend evaporated milk and cornstarch until smooth. Stir into slow cooker. Cover; cook on HIGH 15 to 30 minutes. Just before serving, stir in crabmeat and green onions. *Makes 5 servings*

Rustic Vegetable Soup

1 to 2 baking potatoes, cut in ½-inch pieces
1 jar (16 ounces) picante sauce
1 package (10 ounces) frozen mixed vegetables, thawed
1 package (10 ounces) frozen cut green beans, thawed
1 can (10 ounces) condensed beef broth, undiluted
1 medium green bell pepper, chopped
½ teaspoon sugar
¼ cup finely chopped fresh parsley

Combine all ingredients except parsley in slow cooker. Cover; cook on LOW 8 hours or on HIGH 4 hours. Stir in parsley; serve. *Makes 8 servings*

Potato-Crab Chowder

Minestrone alla Milanese

1 cup diced potato
1 cup coarsely chopped carrots
2 cans (about 14 ounces each) reduced-sodium beef broth
1 can (14½ ounces) diced tomatoes, undrained
1 cup coarsely chopped green cabbage
1 cup sliced zucchini
¾ cup chopped onion
¾ cup sliced fresh green beans
¾ cup coarsely chopped celery
¾ cup water
2 tablespoons olive oil
1 clove garlic, minced
½ teaspoon dried basil leaves
¼ teaspoon dried rosemary
1 bay leaf
1 can (about 15 ounces) cannellini beans, rinsed and drained
Grated Parmesan cheese (optional)

1. Combine all ingredients except cannellini beans and cheese in slow cooker; mix well. Cover; cook on LOW 5 to 6 hours.

2. Add cannellini beans. Cover; cook on LOW 1 hour or until vegetables are crisp-tender.

3. Remove and discard bay leaf. Garnish with cheese, if desired.

Makes 8 to 10 servings

Minestrone alla Milanese

Campfire Sausage and Potato Soup

        8 ounces kielbasa sausage
        1 large baking potato, cut into ½-inch cubes
        1 can (about 15 ounces) dark kidney beans, rinsed and drained
        1 can (14½ ounces) diced tomatoes, undrained
        1 can (10½ ounces) condensed beef broth
        1 medium onion, diced
        1 medium green bell pepper, diced
        1 teaspoon dried oregano leaves
    ½ teaspoon sugar
        1 to 2 teaspoons ground cumin

1. Cut sausage lengthwise in half, then crosswise into ½-inch pieces. Combine potato, sausage, beans, tomatoes with juice, broth, onion, bell pepper, oregano and sugar in slow cooker.

2. Cover; cook on LOW 8 hours or on HIGH 4 hours.

3. Season with cumin before serving.   *Makes 6 to 7 servings*

Slow Cooked Chicken & Wild Rice Soup

        ½ cup uncooked wild rice, rinsed thoroughly
        2 medium carrots, peeled and shredded
        2 stalks celery, thinly sliced
        1 large yellow onion, chopped
    5½ cups water
        2 tablespoons HERB-OX® chicken flavored bouillon
        1 cup heavy whipping cream
        2 tablespoons all-purpose flour
        2 (10-ounce) cans HORMEL® chunk breast of chicken
        Slivered almonds, for garnish

In large (6-quart) slow cooker, combine all ingredients except heavy cream, flour and chunk chicken. Cover and cook on LOW for 4 hours or until rice is tender. Just before serving, combine heavy cream and flour. Slowly stir cream mixture into soup and add chunk chicken. Cook and stir constantly for 5 to 10 minutes or until mixture is slightly thickened and chicken is heated through. Ladle into bowls and garnish with slivered almonds.
                    Makes 6 to 8 servings

Campfire Sausage and Potato Soup

Mediterranean Shrimp Soup

2 cans (about 14 ounces each) reduced-sodium chicken broth
1 can (14½ ounces) diced tomatoes, undrained
1 can (8 ounces) tomato sauce
1 medium onion, chopped
½ medium green bell pepper, chopped
½ cup orange juice
½ cup dry white wine (optional)
1 jar (2½ ounces) sliced mushrooms
¼ cup ripe olives, sliced
2 cloves garlic, minced
1 teaspoon dried basil leaves
2 bay leaves
¼ teaspoon fennel seeds, crushed
⅛ teaspoon black pepper
1 pound uncooked medium shrimp, peeled

Place all ingredients except shrimp in slow cooker. Cover; cook on LOW 4 to 4½ hours or until vegetables are crisp-tender. Stir in shrimp. Cover; cook 15 to 30 minutes or until shrimp are opaque. Remove and discard bay leaves. *Makes 6 servings*

Note: For a heartier soup, add some fish. Cut 1 pound of firm white fish, such as cod or haddock, into 1-inch pieces. Add the fish to the slow cooker 45 minutes before serving. Cover and cook on LOW.

Mediterranean Shrimp Soup

Sausage, Butter Bean and Cabbage Soup

2 tablespoons butter, divided
1 large onion, chopped
12 ounces smoked sausage, such as kielbasa or andouille, cut into
½-inch slices
8 cups chicken broth
½ head savoy cabbage, coarsely shredded
3 tablespoons tomato paste
1 bay leaf
4 medium tomatoes, chopped
2 cans (about 14 ounces each) butter beans, drained
Salt and black pepper

1. Melt 1 tablespoon butter in large skillet over medium heat. Add onion; cook and stir 3 to 4 minutes or until golden. Place in 3½- to 4-quart slow cooker.

2. Melt remaining 1 tablespoon butter in same skillet; cook sausage until brown on both sides. Add to slow cooker.

3. Place chicken broth, cabbage, tomato paste and bay leaf in slow cooker; stir until well blended. Cover; cook on LOW 4 hours or HIGH 2 hours.

4. Add tomatoes and beans; season with salt and pepper. Cover; cook 1 hour until heated through. Remove and discard bay leaf.   *Makes 6 servings*

Tip: Savoy cabbage is an excellent cooking cabbage with a full head of crinkled leaves varying from dark to pale green. Green cabbage may be substituted.

Sausage, Butter Bean and Cabbage Soup

Fiesta Black Bean Soup

6 cups chicken broth
12 ounces potatoes, peeled and diced
1 can (about 15 ounces) black beans, rinsed and drained
½ pound cooked ham, diced
½ onion, diced
1 can (4 ounces) chopped jalapeño peppers
2 cloves garlic, minced
2 teaspoons dried oregano leaves
1½ teaspoons dried thyme leaves
1 teaspoon ground cumin
Toppings: sour cream, chopped bell pepper and chopped tomatoes

1. Combine broth, potatoes, beans, ham, onion, jalapeño peppers, garlic, oregano, thyme and cumin in slow cooker; mix well.

2. Cover; cook on LOW 8 to 10 hours or on HIGH 4 to 5 hours.

3. Adjust seasonings. Serve with desired toppings.   *Makes 6 to 8 servings*

Vegetable and Red Lentil Soup

1 can (about 14 ounces) vegetable broth
1 can (14½ ounces) diced tomatoes, undrained
2 medium zucchini or yellow summer squash (or 1 of each), diced
1 red or yellow bell pepper, diced
½ cup thinly sliced carrots
½ cup red lentils, sorted and rinsed*
½ teaspoon salt
½ teaspoon sugar
¼ teaspoon freshly ground black pepper
2 tablespoons chopped fresh basil or thyme
½ cup croutons or shredded cheese (optional)

*If you have difficulty finding red lentils, substitute brown lentils instead.

Coat slow cooker with cooking spray. Combine broth, tomatoes, squash, bell pepper, carrots, lentils, salt, sugar and pepper in slow cooker; mix well. Cover; cook on LOW 8 hours or on HIGH 4 hours, or until lentils and vegetables are tender. Ladle into shallow bowls; top with basil and croutons, if desired.   *Makes 4 servings*

Fiesta Black Bean Soup

Creamy Slow Cooker Seafood Chowder

1 quart (4 cups) half-and-half
2 cans (about 15 ounces each) whole white potatoes, drained and cubed
2 cans (10¾ ounces) condensed cream of mushroom soup, undiluted
1 bag (16 ounces) frozen hash brown potatoes, thawed
1 medium onion, minced
½ cup (1 stick) butter, diced
1 teaspoon salt
1 teaspoon black pepper
5 cans (about 8 ounces each) whole oysters, drained and rinsed
2 cans (about 6 ounces each) minced clams
2 cans (about 4 ounces each) cocktail shrimp, drained and rinsed

1. Combine half-and-half, canned potatoes, soup, potatoes, onion, butter, salt and pepper in 5- or 6-quart slow cooker. Mix well.

2. Add oysters, clams and shrimp; stir gently.

3. Cover; cook on LOW 4 to 5 hours. *Makes 8 to 10 servings*

Navy Bean & Ham Soup

6 cups water
5 cups dried navy beans, soaked overnight and drained
1 pound ham, cubed
1 can (15 ounces) corn, drained
1 can (4 ounces) mild diced green chilies, drained
1 onion, diced
Salt and black pepper to taste

Place all ingredients in slow cooker. Cover; cook on LOW 8 to 10 hours or until beans are softened. *Makes 6 servings*

Creamy Slow Cooker Seafood Chowder

Smoked Sausage Gumbo

1 can (14½ ounces) diced tomatoes, undrained
1 cup chicken broth
¼ cup all-purpose flour
2 tablespoons olive oil
¾ pound Polish sausage, cut into ½-inch pieces
1 medium onion, diced
1 green bell pepper, diced
2 ribs celery, chopped
1 carrot, peeled and chopped
2 teaspoons dried oregano leaves
2 teaspoons dried thyme leaves
⅛ teaspoon ground red pepper
**   Hot cooked rice**
**   Chopped parsley (optional)**

1. Combine tomatoes with juice and broth in slow cooker. Sprinkle flour evenly over bottom of small skillet. Cook over high heat without stirring 3 to 4 minutes or until flour begins to brown. Reduce heat to medium; stir flour about 4 minutes. Stir in oil until smooth. Carefully whisk flour mixture into slow cooker.

2. Add sausage, onion, bell pepper, celery, carrot, oregano, thyme and red pepper to slow cooker. Stir well. Cover; cook on LOW 4½ to 5 hours.

3. Serve gumbo over rice. Sprinkle with parsley, if desired.   *Makes 4 servings*

Tip: If gumbo thickens upon standing, stir in additional broth.

Smoked Sausage Gumbo

Potato and Leek Soup

4 cups chicken broth
3 potatoes, peeled and diced
1½ cups chopped cabbage
1 leek, diced
1 onion, chopped
2 carrots, diced
¼ cup chopped fresh parsley
1 teaspoon salt
½ teaspoon caraway seeds
½ teaspoon black pepper
1 bay leaf
½ cup sour cream
1 pound bacon, crisp-cooked and crumbled

1. Combine broth, potatoes, cabbage, leek, onion, carrots, parsley, salt, caraway seeds, pepper and bay leaf in slow cooker; mix well.

2. Cover; cook on LOW 8 to 10 hours or on HIGH 4 to 5 hours.

3. Remove and discard bay leaf. Combine ½ cup hot liquid from slow cooker with sour cream in small bowl. Add mixture and bacon to slow cooker; mix well.

Makes 6 to 8 servings

Helpful Hint

Sour cream has a tendency to curdle when subjected to hot liquid. Be sure to whisk a little of the hot liquid into the sour cream, then stir the sour cream mixture into the contents of the slow cooker.

Potato and Leek Soup

Easy Corn Chowder

2 cans (about 14 ounces each) chicken broth
1 bag (16 ounces) frozen corn kernels, thawed
3 small potatoes, peeled and cut into ½-inch pieces
1 red bell pepper, diced
1 medium onion, diced
1 rib celery, sliced
½ teaspoon salt
½ teaspoon black pepper
¼ teaspoon ground coriander
½ cup heavy cream
8 slices bacon, crisp-cooked and crumbled

1. Place broth, corn, potatoes, bell pepper, onion, celery, salt, black pepper and coriander into slow cooker. Cover; cook on LOW 7 to 8 hours.

2. Partially mash soup mixture with potato masher to thicken. Stir in cream; cook on HIGH, uncovered, until hot. Adjust seasonings, if desired. Garnish with bacon.

Makes 6 servings

Prep Time: 15 minutes
Cook Time: 7 to 8 hours

Easy Corn Chowder

Easy Vegetarian Vegetable Bean Soup

3 cans (14 ounces each) vegetable broth
2 cups cubed unpeeled potatoes
2 cups sliced leeks, white part only (about 3 medium)
1 can (14½ ounces) diced tomatoes, undrained
1 medium onion, chopped
1 cup chopped or shredded cabbage
1 cup sliced celery
1 cup sliced peeled carrots
3 cloves garlic, chopped
⅛ teaspoon dried rosemary
1 can (about 16 ounces) Great Northern beans, drained
Salt and black pepper

1. Combine broth, potatoes, leeks, tomatoes, onion, cabbage, celery, carrots, garlic and rosemary in slow cooker.

2. Cover; cook on LOW 8 hours.

3. Stir in beans and season with salt and pepper. Cover; cook about 30 minutes or until beans are heated through. *Makes 10 servings*

Easy Vegetarian Vegetable Bean Soup

Homestyle Chilis

Great Chili

1½ **pounds ground beef**
1½ **cups chopped onion**
1 **cup chopped green bell pepper**
2 **cloves garlic, minced**
3 **cans (about 15 ounces each) dark red kidney beans, rinsed and drained**
2 **cans (15 ounces each) tomato sauce**
1 **can (14½ ounces) diced tomatoes, undrained**
2 to 3 **teaspoons chili powder**
1 to 2 **teaspoons dry hot mustard**
¾ **teaspoon dried basil leaves**
½ **teaspoon black pepper**
1 to 2 **dried hot chili peppers (optional)**

1. Cook and stir ground beef, onion, bell pepper and garlic in large skillet until meat is browned and onion is tender. Drain. Place beef mixture in 5-quart slow cooker.

2. Add beans, tomato sauce, tomatoes with juice, chili powder, mustard, basil, black pepper and chili pepper, if desired; mix well.

3. Cover; cook on LOW 8 to 10 hours or on HIGH 4 to 5 hours. Remove chili pepper, if desired, before serving. *Makes 6 servings*

Great Chili

1-2-3 Chili

2 pounds ground beef
4 cans (8 ounces each) tomato sauce
3 cans (about 15 ounces each) chili beans in mild or spicy sauce, undrained
Shredded Cheddar cheese
Sliced green onions

1. Brown beef in large nonstick skillet over medium-high heat, stirring to break up meat. Drain. Combine beef, tomato sauce and beans with sauce in slow cooker; mix well.

2. Cover; cook on LOW 6 to 8 hours.

3. Serve with cheese and green onions.   *Makes 8 servings*

Chicken and Black Bean Chili

1 pound boneless, skinless chicken thighs, cut into 1-inch chunks
2 teaspoons chili powder
2 teaspoons ground cumin
¾ teaspoon salt
1 green bell pepper, diced
1 small onion, chopped
3 cloves garlic, minced
1 can (14½ ounces) diced tomatoes, undrained
1 cup chunky salsa
1 can (about 16 ounces) black beans, rinsed and drained
Optional toppings: sour cream, diced ripe avocado, shredded Cheddar cheese, sliced green onions or chopped cilantro, crushed tortilla or corn chips

1. Coat slow cooker with cooking spray. Combine chicken, chili powder, cumin and salt in slow cooker, tossing to coat. Add bell pepper, onion and garlic; mix well. Stir in tomatoes with juice and salsa. Cover; cook on LOW 5 to 6 hours or on HIGH 2½ to 3 hours, or until chicken is tender.

2. Turn heat to HIGH; stir in beans. Cover and cook 5 to 10 minutes or until beans are heated through. Ladle into shallow bowls; serve with desired toppings.
Makes 4 servings

Double-Hearty, Double-Quick Veggie Chili

2 cans (about 15 ounces each) dark kidney beans, rinsed and drained
1 package (16 ounces) frozen bell pepper stir-fry mixture, thawed, *or* 2 bell peppers,* chopped
1 can (14½ ounces) diced tomatoes with peppers, celery and onions
1 cup frozen corn kernels, thawed
3 tablespoons chili powder
2 teaspoons sugar
2 teaspoons ground cumin, divided
1 tablespoon olive oil
½ teaspoon salt
Sour cream
Chopped cilantro leaves

*If using fresh bell peppers, add 1 small onion, chopped.

1. Combine beans, bell peppers, tomatoes, corn, chili powder, sugar and 1½ teaspoons cumin in slow cooker; mix well.

2. Cover; cook on LOW 6 hours or on HIGH 3 hours.

3. Stir in olive oil, salt and remaining ½ teaspoon cumin. Serve with sour cream and cilantro. *Makes 4 to 6 servings*

Note: If using fresh bell peppers, add 1 small onion, chopped.

Double-Hearty, Double-Quick Veggie Chili

Chunky Chili

   1 pound 90% lean ground beef
   1 medium onion, chopped
   2 cans (14½ ounces each) diced tomatoes, undrained
   1 can (about 15 ounces) pinto beans, rinsed and drained
  ½ cup prepared salsa
   1 tablespoon chili powder
1½ teaspoons ground cumin
    Salt and black pepper
  ½ cup (2 ounces) shredded Cheddar cheese
   3 tablespoons sour cream
    Sliced black olives

1. Cook and stir beef and onions in large skillet over medium-high heat until beef is browned and onion is tender. Drain fat. Place beef mixture, tomatoes with juice, beans, salsa, chili powder and cumin in slow cooker; stir.

2. Cover; cook on LOW 5 to 6 hours or until flavors are blended and chili is bubbly. Season with salt and pepper to taste. Serve with cheese, sour cream and olives.

Makes 4 (1½-cup) servings

Black and White Chili

    Nonstick cooking spray
   1 pound chicken tenders, cut into ¾-inch pieces
   1 cup coarsely chopped onion
   1 can (about 15 ounces) Great Northern beans, drained
   1 can (about 15 ounces) black beans, drained
   1 can (14½ ounces) Mexican-style stewed tomatoes, undrained
   2 tablespoons Texas-style chili powder seasoning mix

1. Spray large saucepan with cooking spray; heat over medium heat until hot. Add chicken and onion; cook and stir 5 minutes or until chicken is browned.

2. Combine chicken mixture, beans, tomatoes with juice and chili seasoning in slow cooker. Cover; cook on LOW 4 to 4½ hours. *Makes 6 servings*

Serving Suggestion: For a change of pace, this delicious chili is excellent served over cooked rice or pasta.

Chunky Chili

Chili

3 pounds cooked ground beef
2 cans (14½ ounces each) diced tomatoes
2 cans (about 14 ounces each) chili beans, undiluted
2 cups sliced onions
1 can (12 ounces) corn, drained
1 cup chopped green bell pepper
1 can tomato sauce
3 tablespoons chili powder
1 teaspoon garlic powder
½ teaspoon ground cumin
½ teaspoon oregano leaves

1. Brown beef in batches in 12-inch skillet over medium-high heat, stirring to break up meat. Drain. Place in 5-quart slow cooker.

2. Add remaining ingredients to slow cooker. Cover; cook on LOW 4 to 5 hours or until onions are tender. *Makes 6 servings*

Chunky Vegetable Chili

1 medium onion, chopped
2 ribs celery, diced
1 carrot, diced
3 cloves garlic, minced
2 cans (about 15 ounces each) Great Northern beans, rinsed and drained
1 cup water
1 cup frozen corn
1 can (6 ounces) tomato paste
1 can (4 ounces) diced mild green chilies, undrained
1 tablespoon chili powder
2 teaspoons dried oregano leaves
1 teaspoon salt

Combine all ingredients in slow cooker. Cover; cook on LOW 5½ to 6 hours or until vegetables are tender. *Makes 6 servings*

Chili

Easy Slow-Cooked Chili

2 pounds lean ground beef
2 tablespoons chili powder
1 tablespoon ground cumin
1 can (28 ounces) crushed tomatoes in purée, undrained
1 can (15 ounces) red kidney beans, drained and rinsed
1 cup water
2 cups _French's_® French Fried Onions,* divided
¼ cup _Frank's_® _RedHot_® Original Cayenne Pepper Sauce
** Sour cream and shredded Cheddar cheese**

*For added Cheddar flavor, substitute **French's® Cheddar French Fried Onions** for the original flavor.*

1. Cook ground beef, chili powder and cumin in large nonstick skillet over medium heat until browned, stirring frequently; drain. Transfer to slow cooker.

2. Stir in tomatoes with juice, beans, water, ½ cup French Fried Onions and **Frank's RedHot** Sauce.

3. Cover; cook on LOW for 6 hours (or on HIGH for 3 hours). Serve chili topped with sour cream, cheese and remaining onions. *Makes 8 servings*

Prep Time: 10 minutes
Cook Time: 6 hours

Easy Slow-Cooked Chili

Three-Bean Turkey Chili

1 pound ground turkey
1 small onion, chopped
1 can (28 ounces) diced tomatoes, undrained
1 can (about 15 ounces) chick-peas, rinsed and drained
1 can (about 15 ounces) kidney beans, rinsed and drained
1 can (about 15 ounces) black beans, rinsed and drained
1 can (8 ounces) tomato sauce
1 can (about 4 ounces) diced mild green chilies
1 to 2 tablespoons chili powder

1. Cook and stir turkey and onion in medium skillet over medium-high heat until turkey is no longer pink, stirring to break up meat. Drain. Place turkey mixture into slow cooker.

2. Add remaining ingredients and mix well. Cover; cook on HIGH 6 to 8 hours.

Makes 6 to 8 servings

White Bean Chili

Nonstick cooking spray
1 pound ground chicken
3 cups coarsely chopped celery
1 can (about 16 ounces) whole tomatoes, undrained and coarsely chopped
1 can (about 15 ounces) Great Northern beans, drained and rinsed
1½ cups coarsely chopped onions
1 cup chicken broth
3 cloves garlic, minced
4 teaspoons chili powder
1½ teaspoons ground cumin
¾ teaspoon ground allspice
¾ teaspoon ground cinnamon
½ teaspoon black pepper

1. Spray large nonstick skillet with nonstick cooking spray. Brown chicken over medium-high heat, stirring to break up chicken.

2. Combine chicken, celery, tomatoes with juice, beans, onions, broth, garlic, chili powder, cumin, allspice, cinnamon and pepper in slow cooker. Cover; cook on LOW 5½ to 6 hours or until celery is tender.

Makes 6 servings

Three-Bean Turkey Chili

Chili with Chocolate

1 pound 90% lean ground beef
1 medium onion, chopped
3 cloves garlic, minced and divided
1 can (28 ounces) diced tomatoes, undrained
1 can (about 15 ounces) chili beans in mild or spicy sauce,
 undrained
2 tablespoons chili powder
1 tablespoon grated semisweet baking chocolate
1 ½ teaspoons ground cumin
½ teaspoon salt
½ teaspoon black pepper
½ teaspoon hot pepper sauce

1. Cook and stir beef, onion and 1 clove garlic in large nonstick skillet over medium-high heat, stirring to break up meat. Drain.

2. Place beef mixture in slow cooker. Add tomatoes with juice, beans with sauce, chili powder, remaining 2 cloves garlic and chocolate; mix well.

3. Cover; cook on LOW 5 to 6 hours. Add cumin, salt, pepper and hot sauce during last 1 hour of cooking. *Makes 4 servings*

Helpful Hint

The chocolate added to this chili pairs well with onions, garlic and chili to contribute richness but not sweetness.

Chili with Chocolate

Cajun Chili

1½ pounds ground beef
2 cans (15 ounces each) Cajun-style mixed vegetables, undrained
2 cans (10¾ ounces each) condensed tomato soup, undiluted
1 can (14½ ounces) diced tomatoes, undrained
3 fully-cooked sausages with Cheddar cheese (about 8 ounces),
quartered and sliced into bite-size pieces

1. Brown ground beef in large nonstick over medium-high heat, stirring to break up beef. Drain. Place ground beef, mixed vegetables, soup, tomatoes with juice and sausages in slow cooker.

2. Cover; cook on HIGH 2 to 3 hours. Serve with shredded Cheddar cheese, if desired.   *Makes 10 servings*

Turkey Chili

20 ounces JENNIE-O TURKEY STORE® Extra Lean Ground Turkey Breast
2 tablespoons chili powder
1 cup diced onions
10 ounces package shredded carrots
2 green peppers, diced
2 zucchini, diced
2 yellow squash, diced
6 cups water
2 tablespoons HERB-OX® Beef Bouillon Granules
28 ounces can diced tomatoes
15 ounces can black beans, drained and rinsed
15 ounces can kidney beans, drained and rinsed
24 ounces jar salsa

Brown and crumble ground turkey in large nonstick pan coated with vegetable spray. Add vegetables to pan and cook for about 5 minutes or until onions are tender. Place turkey and vegetables in large slow cooker along with water, beef granules, diced tomatoes, salsa and beans. Cover and heat mixture on LOW for 4 hours.

Makes 20 servings

Prep Time: 30 minutes
Cook Time: 4 hours

Cajun Chili

Vegetarian Chili

1 tablespoon vegetable oil
1 cup finely chopped onion
1 cup chopped red bell pepper
2 tablespoons minced jalapeño pepper*
1 clove garlic, minced
1 can (about 28 ounces) crushed tomatoes
1 can (about 15 ounces) black beans, rinsed and drained
1 can (about 15 ounces) garbanzo beans, rinsed and drained
½ cup corn
¼ cup tomato paste
1 teaspoon sugar
1 teaspoon ground cumin
1 teaspoon dried basil leaves
1 teaspoon chili powder
¼ teaspoon black pepper
Sour cream and shredded Cheddar cheese (optional)

*Jalapeño peppers can sting and irritate the skin. Wear rubber gloves when handling peppers and do not touch your eyes. Wash hands after handling peppers.

1. Heat oil in large nonstick skillet over medium-high heat until hot. Add onion, bell pepper, jalapeño pepper and garlic; cook and stir 5 minutes or until vegetables are tender.

2. Transfer vegetables to slow cooker. Add remaining ingredients except sour cream and cheese; mix well. Cover; cook on LOW 4 to 5 hours. Garnish with sour cream and cheese, if desired. *Makes 4 servings*

Vegetarian Chili

Easy Side Dishes

Peasant Potatoes

¼ cup (½ stick) butter
1 large onion, chopped
2 large cloves garlic, chopped
½ pound smoked beef sausage, cut into ¾-inch slices
1 teaspoon dried oregano leaves
6 medium potatoes, preferably Yukon Gold, cut into 1½ to 2-inch pieces
Salt and black pepper
2 cups sliced Savoy or other cabbage
1 cup diced or sliced roasted red pepper
½ cup shaved Parmesan cheese

1. Melt butter in large skillet over medium heat. Add onion and garlic; cook and stir 5 minutes or until onion is transparent. Stir in sausage and oregano. Cook 5 minutes. Stir in potatoes, salt and black pepper; mix well. Transfer mixture to slow cooker.

2. Cover; cook on LOW 6 to 8 hours or on HIGH 3 to 4 hours. Add cabbage and bell peppers during last 30 minutes of cooking.

3. Top with Parmesan cheese before serving.

Makes 6 servings

Peasant Potatoes

Winter Squash and Apples

1 teaspoon salt
½ teaspoon black pepper
1 butternut squash (about 2 pounds), peeled and seeded
2 apples, cored and cut into slices
1 medium onion, quartered and sliced
1½ tablespoons butter

1. Combine salt and pepper in small bowl; set aside.

2. Cut squash into 2-inch pieces; place in slow cooker. Add apples and onion. Sprinkle with salt mixture; stir well. Cover; cook on LOW 6 to 7 hours or until vegetables are tender.

3. Just before serving, stir in butter and season to taste with additional salt and pepper. *Makes 4 to 6 servings*

Variation: Add ¼ to ½ cup packed brown sugar and ½ teaspoon ground cinnamon with butter in step 3; mix well. Cook an additional 15 minutes.

Prep Time: 15 minutes
Cook Time: 6 to 7 hours

Asparagus and Cheese Side Dish

1½ pounds fresh asparagus, trimmed
2 cups crushed saltine crackers
1 can (10¾ ounces) condensed cream of asparagus soup, undiluted
1 can (10¾ ounces) condensed cream of chicken soup, undiluted
⅔ cup slivered almonds
4 ounces American cheese, cut into cubes
1 egg

Combine all ingredients in large bowl; stir well. Pour into slow cooker. Cover; cook on HIGH 3 to 3½ hours or until asparagus is tender. Garnish as desired.
Makes 4 to 6 servings

Winter Squash and Apples

Spinach Spoon Bread

**1 package (10 ounces) frozen chopped spinach, thawed and
   squeezed dry**
1 red bell pepper, diced
4 eggs, lightly beaten
1 cup cottage cheese
1 package (5½ ounces) cornbread mix
6 green onions, sliced
½ cup butter, melted
1¼ teaspoons seasoned salt

1. Lightly grease slow cooker insert; preheat on HIGH.

2. Combine all ingredients in large bowl; mix well. Pour batter into slow cooker. Cook, covered with lid slightly ajar to allow excess moisture to escape, on HIGH 1¾ to 2 hours or on LOW 3 to 4 hours or until edges are golden and knife inserted in center of bread comes out clean.

3. Serve bread spooned from slow cooker. Or, loosen edges and bottom of bread with knife and invert onto plate. Cut into wedges to serve.   *Makes 8 servings*

Mexican-Style Rice and Cheese

1 can (about 15 ounces) Mexican-style beans
**1 can (14½ ounces) diced tomatoes with jalapeño peppers,
   undrained**
2 cups (8 ounces) shredded Monterey Jack or Colby cheese, divided
1½ cups uncooked converted long-grain rice
1 large onion, finely chopped
½ package (4 ounces) cream cheese
3 cloves garlic, minced

1. Grease inside of slow cooker. Combine beans, tomatoes with juice, 1 cup cheese, rice, onion, cream cheese and garlic in slow cooker; mix well.

2. Cover; cook on LOW 6 to 8 hours.

3. Sprinkle with remaining 1 cup cheese just before serving.

Makes 6 to 8 servings

Spinach Spoon bread

Rustic Cheddar Mashed Potatoes

2 pounds russet potatoes, peeled and diced
1 cup water
⅓ cup butter, cut into small pieces
½ to ¾ cup milk
1¼ teaspoons salt
½ teaspoon black pepper
½ cup finely chopped green onions
½ to ¾ cup (2 to 3 ounces) shredded Cheddar cheese

1. Combine potatoes and water in slow cooker; dot with butter. Cover; cook on LOW 6 hours or on HIGH 3 hours or until potatoes are tender.

2. Whip potatoes with electric mixer at medium setting until well blended. Add milk, salt and pepper; whip until well blended.

3. Stir in green onions and cheese. Cover; let stand 15 minutes to allow flavors to blend and cheese to melt. *Makes 8 servings*

Easy Holiday Stuffing

1 cup butter, melted
2 cups chopped celery
1 cup chopped onion
1 teaspoon poultry seasoning
1 teaspoon leaf sage, crumbled
½ teaspoon ground black pepper
3 tablespoons HERB-OX® chicken flavored bouillon
2 eggs, beaten
2 cups water
12 cups dry breadcrumbs

In large bowl, combine butter, celery, onion, spices, bouillon, eggs and water together. Add breadcrumbs and stir to blend. Place mixture in slow cooker. Cook on HIGH for 45 minutes; reduce heat to LOW and heat for 6 hours (or cook on HIGH for 3 hours). *Makes 12 servings*

Prep Time: 10 minutes
Total Time: 3¾ to 6¾ hours

Rustic Cheddar Mashed Potatoes

Red Cabbage and Apples

1 small head red cabbage, cored and thinly sliced
3 medium apples, peeled and grated
¾ cup sugar
½ cup red wine vinegar
1 teaspoon ground cloves
1 cup crisp-cooked and crumbled bacon (optional)

Combine cabbage, apples, sugar, red wine vinegar and cloves in slow cooker.
Cover; cook on HIGH 6 hours, stirring after 3 hours. Sprinkle with bacon, if desired.
Garnish as desired.   *Makes 4 to 6 servings*

Bean Pot Medley

1 can (about 15 ounces) black beans, rinsed and drained
1 can (about 15 ounces) red beans, rinsed and drained
1 can (about 15 ounces) Great Northern beans, rinsed and drained
1 can (about 15 ounces) black-eyed peas, rinsed and drained
1 can (about 8 ounces) baby lima beans, rinsed and drained
1½ cups ketchup
1 cup chopped onion
1 cup chopped red bell pepper
1 cup chopped green bell pepper
½ cup packed brown sugar
½ cup water
2 to 3 teaspoons cider vinegar
1 teaspoon dry mustard
2 bay leaves
⅛ teaspoon black pepper

1. Combine beans, ketchup, onion, bell peppers, brown sugar, water, vinegar,
mustard, bay leaves and black pepper in 3½- to 4-quart slow cooker; stir until well
blended.

2. Cover; cook on LOW 6 to 7 hours or until onion and bell peppers are tender.

3. Remove and discard bay leaves.   *Makes 8 servings*

Red Cabbage and Apples

Scalloped Potatoes and Parsnips

        6 tablespoons unsalted butter
        3 tablespoons all-purpose flour
      1¾ cups heavy cream
        2 teaspoons dry mustard
      1½ teaspoons salt
        1 teaspoon dried thyme leaves
        ½ teaspoon black pepper
        2 baking potatoes, cut in half lengthwise, then crosswise into
              ¼-inch slices
        2 parsnips, cut into ¼-inch slices
        1 onion, chopped
        2 cups (8 ounces) shredded sharp Cheddar cheese

1. To prepare cream sauce, melt butter in medium saucepan over medium-high heat. Stir in flour; cook and stir 3 to 5 minutes. Slowly whisk in cream, mustard, salt, thyme and pepper until smooth.

2. Arrange potatoes, parsnips and onion in slow cooker. Add cream sauce.

3. Cover; cook on LOW 7 hours or on HIGH 3½ hours or until potatoes are tender. Stir in cheese. Cover; let stand until cheese melts.   *Makes 4 to 6 servings*

Helpful Hint

Baking potatoes, sometimes referred to as russet or Idaho potatoes, have a high starch content, which helps potato slices in scalloped dishes hold their shape.

Scalloped Potatoes and Parsnips

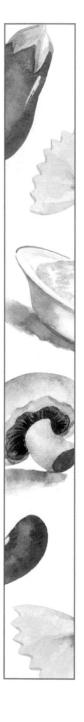

Spanish Paella-Style Rice

2 cans (about 14 ounces each) chicken broth
1½ cups uncooked converted long-grain rice
1 small red bell pepper, diced
⅓ cup dry white wine or water
½ teaspoon saffron threads, crushed, *or* ½ teaspoon ground turmeric
⅛ teaspoon red pepper flakes
½ cup frozen peas, thawed
Salt

1. Combine broth, rice, bell pepper, wine, saffron and pepper flakes in 2½-quart slow cooker; mix well.

2. Cover; cook on LOW 4 hours or until liquid is absorbed.

3. Stir in peas. Cover; cook 15 to 30 minutes or until peas are hot. Season with salt.

Makes 6 servings

Note: Saffron is a very expensive spice, which tints dishes a yellow color as well as flavors them. Tumeric is a less expensive spice that produces the characteristic color but not the flavor of saffron. When purchasing saffron look for saffron threads rather than ground saffron because the threads retain their flavor longer.

Variations: Add ½ cup cooked chicken, ham or shrimp or quartered marinated artichokes, drained, with peas.

Prep Time: 10 minutes
Cook Time: 4½ hours

Spanish Paella-Style Rice

Cran-Orange Acorn Squash

3 small acorn or carnival squash
5 tablespoons instant brown rice
3 tablespoons minced onion
3 tablespoons diced celery
3 tablespoons dried cranberries
   Pinch ground or dried sage leaves
1 teaspoon butter, cut into bits
3 tablespoons orange juice
½ cup water

1. Cut off tops of squash and enough of bottoms so they will sit upright. Scoop out seeds and discard; set squash aside.

2. Combine rice, onion, celery, cranberries and sage in small bowl. Stuff each squash with rice mixture; dot with butter. Pour 1 tablespoon orange juice into each squash over stuffing. Stand squash in slow cooker. Pour water into bottom of slow cooker.

3. Cover; cook on LOW 2½ hours or until squash are tender.   *Makes 6 servings*

Tip: The skin of squash can defy even the sharpest knives. To make cutting easier, microwave the whole squash at HIGH 5 minutes to soften the skin.

Cran-Orange Acorn Squash

Sweet-Spiced Sweet Potatoes

2 pounds sweet potatoes, peeled and cut into ½-inch pieces
¼ cup packed dark brown sugar
1 teaspoon ground cinnamon
½ teaspoon ground nutmeg
⅛ teaspoon salt
2 tablespoons butter, cut into ⅛-inch pieces
1 teaspoon vanilla

Combine all ingredients except butter and vanilla in slow cooker; mix well. Cover; cook on LOW 7 hours or on HIGH 4 hours. Add butter and vanilla; stir to blend.

Makes 4 servings

Spicy Beans Tex-Mex

⅓ cup lentils
1⅓ cups water
5 strips bacon
1 onion, chopped
1 can (about 15 ounces) pinto beans, rinsed and drained
1 can (about 15 ounces) red kidney beans, rinsed and drained
1 can (14½ ounces) diced tomatoes, undrained
3 tablespoons ketchup
3 cloves garlic, minced
1 teaspoon chili powder
½ teaspoon ground cumin
¼ teaspoon red pepper flakes
1 bay leaf

1. Boil lentils in water 20 to 30 minutes in large saucepan; drain. Cook bacon in medium skillet until crisp. Remove to paper towels. Cool and crumble bacon. In same skillet, cook onion in bacon drippings until soft.

2. Combine lentils, bacon, onion, beans, tomatoes with juice, ketchup, garlic, chili powder, cumin, pepper flakes and bay leaf in slow cooker.

3. Cover; cook on LOW 5 to 6 hours or on HIGH 3 to 4 hours. Remove bay leaf before serving.

Makes 8 to 10 servings

Prep Time: 35 minutes
Cook Time: 5 to 6 hours

Sweet-Spiced Sweet Potatoes

Green Bean Casserole

2 packages (10 ounces each) frozen green beans, thawed
1 can (10½ ounces) condensed cream of mushroom soup, undiluted
1 tablespoon chopped fresh parsley
1 tablespoon chopped roasted red peppers
1 teaspoon dried sage leaves
½ teaspoon salt
½ teaspoon black pepper
¼ teaspoon ground nutmeg
½ cup toasted slivered almonds

Combine all ingredients except almonds in 2½-quart slow cooker. Cover; cook on LOW 3 to 4 hours. Sprinkle with almonds. *Makes 4 to 6 servings*

Sweet Potato & Pecan Casserole

1 can (40 ounces) sweet potatoes, drained and mashed
½ cup apple juice
⅓ cup plus 2 tablespoons butter, melted, divided
½ teaspoon salt
½ teaspoon ground cinnamon
¼ teaspoon black pepper
2 eggs, beaten
⅓ cup chopped pecans
⅓ cup brown sugar
2 tablespoons all-purpose flour

1. Lightly grease slow cooker. Combine sweet potatoes, apple juice, ⅓ cup butter, salt, cinnamon and pepper in large bowl. Beat in eggs. Place mixture into prepared slow cooker.

2. Combine pecans, brown sugar, flour and remaining 2 tablespoons butter in small bowl. Spread over sweet potatoes.

3. Cover; cook on HIGH 3 to 4 hours. *Makes 6 to 8 servings*

Tip: This casserole is excellent to make for the holidays. Using the slow cooker frees the oven for other dishes.

Green Bean Casserole

Mediterranean Red Potatoes

3 medium red potatoes, cut in half lengthwise, then crosswise into pieces
⅔ cup fresh or frozen pearl onions
Nonstick garlic-flavored cooking spray
¾ teaspoon dried Italian seasoning
¼ teaspoon black pepper
1 small tomato, seeded and chopped
2 ounces (½ cup) feta cheese, crumbled
2 tablespoons chopped black olives

1. Place potatoes and onions in 1½-quart soufflé dish. Spray potatoes and onions with cooking spray; toss to coat. Add Italian seasoning and pepper; mix well. Cover dish tightly with foil.

2. Tear off 3 (18×3-inch) strips of heavy-duty foil. Cross strips to resemble wheel spokes. (See page 15.) Place soufflé dish in center of strips. Pull foil strips up and over dish and place dish into slow cooker.

3. Pour hot water into slow cooker to about 1½ inches from top of soufflé dish. Cover; cook on LOW 7 to 8 hours.

4. Use foil handles to lift dish out of slow cooker. Stir tomato, feta cheese and olives into potato mixture. *Makes 4 servings*

Mediterranean Red Potatoes

Risotto-Style Peppered Rice

1 cup uncooked converted long-grain rice
1 medium green bell pepper, chopped
1 medium red bell pepper, chopped
1 cup chopped onion
½ teaspoon ground turmeric
⅛ teaspoon ground red pepper (optional)
1 can (14 ounces) chicken broth
4 ounces Monterey Jack cheese with jalapeño peppers, cubed
½ cup milk
¼ cup (½ stick) butter, cubed
1 teaspoon salt

1. Place rice, bell peppers, onion, turmeric and ground red pepper, if desired, in slow cooker. Stir in broth.

2. Cover; cook on LOW 4 to 5 hours or until rice is tender and broth is absorbed.

3. Stir in cheese, milk, butter and salt; fluff rice with fork. Cover; cook on LOW 5 minutes or until cheese melts.   *Makes 4 to 6 servings*

Helpful Hint

Converted long-grain rice is better suited for use in slow cookers. It tends to retain its shape and is less likely to become mushy with long cooking.

Risotto-Style Peppered Rice

Orange-Spiced Sweet Potatoes

2 pounds sweet potatoes, peeled and diced
½ cup dark brown sugar, packed
½ cup butter (1 stick), cut in small pieces
1 teaspoon ground cinnamon
½ teaspoon ground nutmeg
½ teaspoon grated orange peel
Juice of 1 medium orange
¼ teaspoon salt
1 teaspoon vanilla
Chopped toasted pecans (optional)

Place all ingredients in slow cooker, except pecans. Cover; cook on LOW 4 hours or on HIGH 2 hours or until potatoes are tender. Sprinkle with pecans before serving, if desired. *Makes 8 (½-cup) servings*

Variation: Mash sweet potatoes with a hand masher or electric mixer; add ¼ cup milk or whipping cream for a moister consistency. Sprinkle with a mixture of sugar and cinnamon.

Risi Bisi

1½ cups converted long-grain white rice
¾ cup chopped onion
2 cloves garlic, minced
2 cans (about 14 ounces each) chicken broth
⅓ cup water
¾ teaspoon Italian seasoning
½ teaspoon dried basil leaves
½ cup frozen peas
¼ cup grated Parmesan cheese
¼ cup toasted pine nuts (optional)

1. Combine rice, onion and garlic in slow cooker. Heat broth and water in small saucepan to a boil. Stir boiling broth mixture, Italian seasoning and basil into rice mixture. Cover; cook on LOW 2 to 3 hours or until liquid is absorbed.

2. Add peas. Cover; cook 1 hour. Stir in cheese. Spoon rice into serving bowl. Sprinkle with pine nuts, if desired. *Makes 6 servings*

Orange-Spiced Sweet Potatoes

Garden Potato Casserole

1¼ **pounds baking potatoes, unpeeled, sliced**
  1 **small green or red bell pepper, thinly sliced**
¼ **cup finely chopped yellow onion**
  2 **tablespoons butter, cut into bits, divided**
½ **teaspoon salt**
½ **teaspoon dried thyme leaves**
  Black pepper to taste
  1 **small yellow squash, thinly sliced**
  1 **cup (4 ounces) shredded sharp Cheddar cheese**

1. Place potatoes, bell pepper, onion, 1 tablespoon butter, salt, thyme and black pepper in slow cooker; mix well. Evenly layer squash over potato mixture; add remaining 1 tablespoon butter.

2. Cover; cook on LOW 7 hours or on HIGH 4 hours.

3. Remove potato mixture to serving bowl. Sprinkle with cheese; let stand 2 to 3 minutes or until cheese melts.   *Makes 5 servings*

Rustic Potatoes au Gratin

½ **cup milk**
  1 **can (10¾ ounces) condensed Cheddar cheese soup, undiluted**
  1 **package (8 ounces) cream cheese, softened**
  1 **clove garlic, minced**
¼ **teaspoon ground nutmeg**
⅛ **teaspoon black pepper**
  2 **pounds baking potatoes, cut into ¼-inch slices**
  1 **small onion, thinly sliced**
  Paprika (optional)

1. Heat milk in small saucepan over medium heat until small bubbles form around edge of pan. Remove from heat. Add soup, cream cheese, garlic, nutmeg and pepper. Stir until smooth.

2. Layer ¼ of potatoes and ¼ of onion in bottom of slow cooker. Top with ¼ of soup mixture. Repeat layers 3 times, using remaining potatoes, onion and soup mixture.

3. Cover; cook on LOW 6½ to 7 hours or until potatoes are tender and most of liquid is absorbed. Sprinkle with paprika, if desired.   *Makes 6 servings*

Garden Potato Casserole

Delicious Desserts

Mixed Berry Cobbler

1 package (16 ounces) frozen mixed berries
¾ cup granulated sugar
2 tablespoons quick-cooking tapioca
2 teaspoons grated lemon peel
1½ cups all-purpose flour
½ cup packed brown sugar
2¼ teaspoons baking powder
¼ teaspoon ground nutmeg
¾ cup milk
⅓ cup butter, melted
Ice cream (optional)

1. Stir together berries, granulated sugar, tapioca and lemon peel in slow cooker.

2. Combine flour, brown sugar, baking powder and nutmeg in medium bowl. Add milk and butter; stir just until blended. Drop spoonfuls of dough on top of berry mixture.

3. Cover; cook on LOW 4 hours. Uncover; let stand about 30 minutes. Serve with ice cream, if desired. *Makes 8 servings*

Prep Time: 10 minutes
Cook Time: 4 hours
Stand Time: 30 minutes

Mixed Berry Cobbler

Pumpkin-Cranberry Custard

1 can (30 ounces) pumpkin pie filling
1 can (12 ounces) evaporated milk
1 cup dried cranberries
4 eggs, beaten
1 cup crushed or whole ginger snap cookies (optional)
Whipped cream (optional)

Combine pumpkin, evaporated milk, cranberries and eggs in slow cooker; mix thoroughly. Cover; cook on HIGH 4 to 4½ hours. Serve with crushed or whole ginger snaps and whipped cream, if desired. *Make 4 to 6 servings*

Pineapple Rice Pudding

1 can (20 ounces) crushed pineapple in juice, undrained
1 can (13½ ounces) coconut milk
1 can (12 ounces) nonfat evaporated milk
¾ cup uncooked arborio rice
2 eggs, lightly beaten
¼ cup granulated sugar
¼ cup packed light brown sugar
½ teaspoon ground cinnamon
¼ teaspoon ground nutmeg
¼ teaspoon salt
Whipped topping
Toasted coconut for garnish* (optional)

*To toast coconut, spread evenly on ungreased baking sheet. Toast in preheated 350°F oven 5 to 7 minutes, stirring occasionally, until light golden brown.

1. Place pineapple with juice, coconut milk, evaporated milk, rice, eggs, granulated sugar, brown sugar, cinnamon, nutmeg and salt into slow cooker; mix well. Cover; cook on HIGH 3 to 4 hours or until thickened and rice is tender.

2. Remove cover; stir until blended. Serve warm or chilled with whipped topping. Garnish with coconut, if desired. *Makes about 8 (1 cup) servings*

Prep Time: 10 minutes
Cook Time: 3 to 4 hours

Pumpkin-Cranberry Custard

Peach-Pecan Upside-Down Cake

1 can (about 8 ounces) peach slices
⅓ cup packed brown sugar
2 tablespoons butter or margarine, melted
¼ cup chopped pecans
1 package (16 ounces) pound cake mix, plus ingredients to
prepare mix
½ teaspoon almond extract
Whipped cream (optional)

1. Generously grease 7½-inch bread-and-cake bake pan or casserole dish; set aside.

2. Drain peach slices, reserving 1 tablespoon of juice. Combine reserved peach juice, brown sugar and butter in prepared bake pan. Arrange peach slices on top of brown sugar mixture. Sprinkle with pecans.

3. Prepare cake mix according to package directions; stir in almond extract. Spread over peach mixture. Cover pan. Make foil handles (see page 15) for easier removal of pan from slow cooker. Place pan into slow cooker. Cover; cook on HIGH 3 hours.

4. Use foil handles to remove pan from slow cooker. Cool, uncovered, on wire rack for 10 minutes. Run narrow spatula around sides of pan; invert onto serving plate. Serve warm with whipped cream, if desired. *Makes 10 servings*

Note: Bread-and-cake bake pans are offered by one major slow cooker manufacturer. You can substitute any deep casserole or baking pan that will fit into your slow cooker.

Prep Time: 10 minutes
Cook Time: 3 hours

Peach-Pecan Upside-Down Cake

Baked Fudge Pudding Cake

6 tablespoons unsweetened cocoa powder
¼ cup all-purpose flour
⅛ teaspoon salt
4 eggs
1⅓ cups sugar
1 cup (2 sticks) unsalted butter, melted
1 teaspoon vanilla
Grated peel of 1 orange
½ cup whipping cream
Chopped toasted pecans, whipped cream or vanilla ice cream

1. Spray inside of slow cooker with nonstick cooking spray. Preheat slow cooker on LOW setting. Combine cocoa, flour and salt in small bowl; set aside.

2. Beat eggs with electric mixer on medium-high speed until thickened. Gradually add sugar, beating about 5 minutes or until very thick and pale in color. Mix in butter, vanilla and peel. Stir cocoa mixture into egg mixture. Add cream; mix until blended. Pour batter into slow cooker.

3. Before placing lid on slow cooker, cover opening with paper towel to collect condensation, making sure it does not touch the pudding mixture. (Large slow cookers might require 2 connected paper towels.) Place lid over paper towel. Cook on LOW 3 to 4 hours. (Do not cook on HIGH.) Sprinkle with pecans; serve with whipped cream. Refrigerate leftovers. *Makes 6 to 8 servings*

Note: Store leftover cake in a covered container in the refrigerator. To serve leftover cake, reheat individual servings in the microwave for about 15 seconds. Or, make fudge truffles: roll leftover cake into small balls and dip them into melted chocolate. Let stand until chocolate hardens.

Baked Fudge Pudding Cake

Banana-Rum Custard with Vanilla Wafers

1½ cups milk
3 eggs
½ cup sugar
3 tablespoons dark rum or milk
⅛ teaspoon salt
1 medium banana, sliced ¼ inch thick
15 to 18 vanilla wafers

1. Whisk milk, eggs, sugar, rum and salt in medium bowl. Pour into 1-quart casserole. Do not cover.

2. Add rack to 5-quart slow cooker and pour in 1 cup water. Place casserole on rack. Cover; cook on LOW 3½ to 4 hours.

3. Remove casserole from slow cooker. Spoon custard into individual dessert dishes. Arrange banana slices and wafers over custard. Garnish as desired.

Makes 5 servings

Pear Crunch

1 can (8 ounces) crushed pineapple in juice, undrained
¼ cup pineapple or apple juice
3 tablespoons dried cranberries
1½ teaspoons quick-cooking tapioca
¼ teaspoon vanilla
2 pears, cored and cut into halves
¼ cup granola with almonds

1. Combine all ingredients except pears and granola in slow cooker; mix well. Place pears, cut side down, over pineapple mixture. Cover; cook on LOW 3½ to 4½ hours.

2. Arrange pear halves on serving plates. Spoon pineapple mixture over pear halves. Garnish with granola.

Makes 4 servings

Banana-Rum Custard with Vanilla Wafers

Steamed Pumpkin Cake

1½ cups all-purpose flour
1½ teaspoons baking powder
1½ teaspoons baking soda
  1 teaspoon ground cinnamon
  ½ teaspoon salt
  ¼ teaspoon ground cloves
  ½ cup unsalted butter, melted
  2 cups packed light brown sugar
  3 eggs, beaten
  1 can (15 ounces) solid-pack pumpkin
    Sweetened whipped cream (optional)

1. Grease 2½-quart soufflé dish or baking pan that fits into slow cooker.

2. Combine flour, baking powder, baking soda, cinnamon, salt and cloves in medium bowl; set aside.

3. Beat butter, brown sugar and eggs in large bowl with electric mixer on medium speed until creamy. Beat in pumpkin. Stir in flour mixture. Spoon batter into prepared soufflé dish.

4. Fill slow cooker with 1 inch hot water. Make foil handles (see page 15) to allow for easy removal of soufflé dish. Place soufflé dish into slow cooker. Cover; cook on HIGH 3 to 3½ hours or until wooden toothpick inserted into center comes out clean.

5. Use foil handles to lift dish from slow cooker. Cool on wire rack 15 minutes. Invert cake onto serving platter. Cut into wedges and serve with dollop of whipped cream, if desired. *Makes 12 servings*

Serving Suggestion: Enhance this old-fashioned dense cake with a topping of sautéed apples or pear slices, or a scoop of pumpkin ice cream.

Prep Time: 15 minutes
Cook Time: 3 to 3½ hours

Steamed Pumpkin Cake

Pineapple Daiquiri Sundae

1 pineapple, peeled, cored and cut into ½-inch chunks
½ cup dark rum
½ cup sugar
3 tablespoons lime juice
Peel of 2 limes, cut into strips
1 tablespoon cornstarch or arrowroot

Place all ingredients in slow cooker; mix well. Cover; cook on HIGH 3 to 4 hours. Serve hot over ice cream, pound cake or shortcakes. Garnish with a few fresh raspberries and mint leaves, if desired.   *Makes 4 to 6 servings*

Variation: Substitute 1 can (20 ounces) crushed pineapple, drained, for the fresh pineapple. Cook on HIGH 3 hours.

Warm Spiced Apples and Pears

8 tablespoons unsalted butter
1 vanilla bean
1 cup packed dark brown sugar
½ cup water
½ lemon, sliced and seeds removed
1 cinnamon stick, broken in half
½ teaspoon ground cloves
5 pears, quartered and cored
5 small Granny Smith apples, quartered and cored

1. Melt butter in saucepan over medium heat. Cut vanilla bean in half and scrape out seeds. Add seeds and pod to pan with brown sugar, water, lemon slices, cinnamon stick and cloves. Bring to a boil; cook and stir 1 minute. Remove from heat.

2. Place pears and apples in slow cooker; pour lemon syrup over fruit and mix well. Cover; cook on LOW 3½ to 4 hours or on HIGH 2 hours. Stir halfway through cooking.   *Makes 6 servings*

Serving Suggestions: Serve alone or with whipped cream, sponge cake, pound cake or over ice cream. This also would pair well with baked ham, pork loin roast or roast turkey.

Pineapple Daiquiri Sundae

Peach Cobbler

2 packages (16 ounces each) frozen peaches, thawed and drained
¾ cup plus 1 tablespoon sugar, divided
2 teaspoons ground cinnamon, divided
½ teaspoon ground nutmeg
¾ cup all-purpose flour
6 tablespoons butter, cut into bits
Whipped cream (if desired)

1. Combine peaches, ¾ cup sugar, 1½ teaspoons cinnamon and nutmeg in medium bowl. Place into slow cooker.

2. For topping, combine flour, remaining 1 tablespoon sugar and ½ teaspoon cinnamon in small bowl. Cut in butter with pastry blender or 2 knives until mixture resembles coarse crumbs. Sprinkle over peach mixture. Cover; cook on HIGH 2 hours. Serve with freshly whipped cream, if desired.   *Makes 4 to 6 servings*

Cherry Rice Pudding

1½ cups milk
1 cup hot cooked rice
3 eggs, beaten
½ cup sugar
¼ cup dried cherries or cranberries
½ teaspoon almond extract
¼ teaspoon salt

1. Combine all ingredients in large bowl. Pour mixture into greased 1½-quart casserole. Cover with foil.

2. Add rack to 5-quart slow cooker; add 1 cup water. Place casserole on rack. Cover; cook on LOW 4 to 5 hours. Remove casserole from slow cooker. Cool 15 minutes on wire rack. Serve warm.   *Makes 6 servings*

Peach Cobbler

Fruit & Nut Baked Apples

4 large baking apples, such as Rome Beauty or Jonathan
1 tablespoon lemon juice
⅓ cup chopped dried apricots
⅓ cup chopped walnuts or pecans
3 tablespoons packed light brown sugar
½ teaspoon ground cinnamon
2 tablespoons butter or margarine, melted

1. Scoop out center of each apple, leaving 1½-inch-wide cavity about ½ inch from bottom. Peel top of apple down about 1 inch. Brush peeled edges evenly with lemon juice. Mix apricots, walnuts, brown sugar and cinnamon in small bowl. Add butter; mix well. Spoon mixture evenly into apple cavities.

2. Pour ½ cup water in bottom of slow cooker. Place 2 apples in bottom of cooker. Arrange remaining 2 apples above but not directly on top of bottom apples.

3. Cover; cook on LOW 3 to 4 hours or until apples are tender. Serve warm or at room temperature with caramel ice cream topping, if desired.   *Makes 4 servings*

Helpful Hint

Acidic lemon juice is brushed onto the cut surfaces of apples and pears to prevent them from discoloring when they are exposed to air.

Fruit & Nut Baked Apples

Coconut Rice Pudding

2 cups water
1 cup uncooked converted long-grain rice
1 tablespoon unsalted butter
    Pinch salt
2¼ cups evaporated milk
1 can (14 ounces) cream of coconut
½ cup golden raisins
3 egg yolks, beaten
    Grated peel of 2 limes
1 teaspoon vanilla
    Toasted shredded coconut (optional)

1. Place water, rice, butter and salt in medium saucepan. Bring to a boil over high heat, stirring frequently. Reduce heat to low. Cover; cook 10 to 12 minutes. Remove from heat. Let stand covered 5 minutes.

2. Meanwhile, spray slow cooker with nonstick cooking spray. Add evaporated milk, cream of coconut, raisins, egg yolks, lime peel and vanilla; mix well. Add rice; stir until blended.

3. Cover; cook on LOW 4 hours or on HIGH 2 hours. Stir every 30 minutes, if possible. Pudding will thicken as it cools. Garnish with toasted shredded coconut, if desired. *Makes 6 (¾-cup) servings*

Coconut Rice Pudding

Steamed Southern Sweet Potato Custard

1 can (16 ounces) cut sweet potatoes, drained
1 can (12 ounces) evaporated milk, divided
½ cup packed light brown sugar
2 eggs, lightly beaten
1 teaspoon ground cinnamon
½ teaspoon ground ginger
¼ teaspoon salt
Whipped cream
Ground nutmeg

1. Process sweet potatoes with ¼ cup milk in food processor or blender until smooth. Add remaining milk, brown sugar, eggs, cinnamon, ginger and salt; process until well blended. Pour into ungreased 1-quart soufflé dish. Cover tightly with foil. Crumple large sheet (about 15×12 inches) of foil; place in bottom of slow cooker. Pour 2 cups water over foil. Make foil handles (see page 15) to allow for easy removal of soufflé dish.

2. Transfer dish to slow cooker using foil handles; lay foil strips over top of dish. Cover; cook on HIGH 2½ to 3 hours or until skewer inserted in center comes out clean.

3. Using foil strips, lift dish from slow cooker; transfer to wire rack. Uncover; let stand 30 minutes. Garnish with whipped cream and nutmeg. *Makes 4 servings*

Steamed Southern Sweet Potato Custard

"Peachy Keen" Dessert Treat

1⅓ cups uncooked old-fashioned oats
1 cup granulated sugar
1 cup packed light brown sugar
⅔ cup buttermilk baking mix
2 teaspoons ground cinnamon
½ teaspoon ground nutmeg
2 pounds fresh peaches (about 8 medium), sliced

Combine oats, sugars, baking mix, cinnamon and nutmeg in large bowl. Stir in peaches; mix until well blended. Pour mixture into slow cooker. Cover; cook on LOW 4 to 6 hours. *Makes 8 to 12 servings*

Poached Pears with Raspberry Sauce

4 cups cran-raspberry juice cocktail
2 cups Rhine or Riesling wine
¼ cup sugar
2 cinnamon sticks, broken into halves
4 to 5 firm Bosc or Anjou pears, peeled and cored
1 package (10 ounces) frozen raspberries in syrup, thawed
Fresh berries (optional)

1. Combine juice, wine, sugar and cinnamon stick halves in slow cooker. Submerge pears in juice mixture. Cover; cook on LOW 3½ to 4 hours or until pears are tender. Remove and discard cinnamon sticks.

2. Process raspberries in food processor or blender until smooth; strain and discard seeds. Spoon raspberry sauce onto serving plates; place pears on top of sauce. Garnish with fresh berries, if desired. *Makes 4 to 5 servings*

"Peachy Keen" Dessert Treat

Chocolate Croissant Pudding

1½ cups milk
3 eggs
½ cup sugar
¼ cup unsweetened cocoa powder
½ teaspoon vanilla
¼ teaspoon salt
2 plain croissants, cut into 1-inch pieces
½ cup chocolate chips
Whipped cream

1. Whisk milk, eggs, sugar, cocoa, vanilla and salt in medium bowl.

2. Grease 1-quart casserole. Layer half the croissants, chocolate chips and half the egg mixture in casserole. Repeat layers with remaining croissants and egg mixture.

3. Add rack to 5-quart slow cooker; pour in 1 cup water. Place casserole on rack. Cover; cook on LOW 3 to 4 hours. Remove casserole from slow cooker. Serve warm with whipped cream.   *Makes 6 servings*

Chocolate Croissant Pudding

Cherry Flan

 5 eggs
½ cup sugar
½ teaspoon salt
¾ cup all-purpose flour
 1 can (12 ounces) evaporated milk
 1 teaspoon vanilla
 1 bag (16 ounces) frozen, pitted dark sweet cherries, thawed
  Sweetened whipped cream or cherry vanilla ice cream

1. Grease inside of slow cooker.

2. Beat eggs, sugar and salt in large bowl of electric mixer at high speed until thick and pale in color. Add flour; beat until smooth. Beat in evaporated milk and vanilla.

3. Pour batter into prepared slow cooker. Place cherries evenly over batter. Cover; cook on LOW 3½ to 4 hours or until flan is set. Serve warm with whipped cream.

Makes 6 servings

Serving suggestion: Serve this dessert warm and top it with whipped cream or ice cream. Garnish it with cherries and mint leaves.

Prep Time: 10 minutes
Cook Time: 3½ to 4 hours

Cherry Flan

Luscious Pecan Bread Pudding

3 cups day-old French bread cubes
3 tablespoons chopped pecans, toasted
2¼ cups low-fat (1%) milk
2 eggs, beaten
½ cup sugar
1 teaspoon vanilla
¾ teaspoon ground cinnamon, divided
¾ cup reduced-calorie cranberry juice cocktail
1½ cups frozen pitted tart cherries
2 tablespoons sugar substitute

1. Toss bread cubes and pecans in soufflé dish. Combine milk, eggs, sugar, vanilla and ½ teaspoon cinnamon in large bowl. Pour over bread mixture in soufflé dish. Cover tightly with foil. Make foil handles (see page 15) to allow for easy removal of soufflé dish from slow cooker. Place soufflé dish in slow cooker. Pour hot water into slow cooker to about 1½ inches from top of soufflé dish. Cover; cook on LOW 2 to 3 hours.

2. Meanwhile, combine cranberry juice and remaining ¼ teaspoon cinnamon in small saucepan; stir in frozen cherries. Bring sauce to a boil over medium heat; cook about 5 minutes. Remove from heat. Stir in sugar substitute.

3. Lift soufflé dish from slow cooker with foil handles. Serve bread pudding with cherry sauce. *Makes 6 servings*

Luscious Pecan Bread Pudding

Acknowledgments

The publisher would like to thank the companies and organizations listed below for the use of their recipes and photographs in this publication.

Hormel Foods, LLC

Jennie-O Turkey Store®

Lawry's® Foods

National Pork Board

Reckitt Benckiser Inc.

Index

METRIC CONVERSION CHART

VOLUME MEASUREMENTS (dry)

1/8 teaspoon = 0.5 mL
1/4 teaspoon = 1 mL
1/2 teaspoon = 2 mL
3/4 teaspoon = 4 mL
1 teaspoon = 5 mL
1 tablespoon = 15 mL
2 tablespoons = 30 mL
1/4 cup = 60 mL
1/3 cup = 75 mL
1/2 cup = 125 mL
2/3 cup = 150 mL
3/4 cup = 175 mL
1 cup = 250 mL
2 cups = 1 pint = 500 mL
3 cups = 750 mL
4 cups = 1 quart = 1 L

VOLUME MEASUREMENTS (fluid)

1 fluid ounce (2 tablespoons) = 30 mL
4 fluid ounces (1/2 cup) = 125 mL
8 fluid ounces (1 cup) = 250 mL
12 fluid ounces (1 1/2 cups) = 375 mL
16 fluid ounces (2 cups) = 500 mL

WEIGHTS (mass)

1/2 ounce = 15 g
1 ounce = 30 g
3 ounces = 90 g
4 ounces = 120 g
8 ounces = 225 g
10 ounces = 285 g
12 ounces = 360 g
16 ounces = 1 pound = 450 g

DIMENSIONS

1/16 inch = 2 mm
1/8 inch = 3 mm
1/4 inch = 6 mm
1/2 inch = 1.5 cm
3/4 inch = 2 cm
1 inch = 2.5 cm

OVEN TEMPERATURES

250°F = 120°C
275°F = 140°C
300°F = 150°C
325°F = 160°C
350°F = 180°C
375°F = 190°C
400°F = 200°C
425°F = 220°C
450°F = 230°C

BAKING PAN SIZES

Utensil	Size in Inches/Quarts	Metric Volume	Size in Centimeters
Baking or Cake Pan (square or rectangular)	8 × 8 × 2	2 L	20 × 20 × 5
	9 × 9 × 2	2.5 L	23 × 23 × 5
	12 × 8 × 2	3 L	30 × 20 × 5
	13 × 9 × 2	3.5 L	33 × 23 × 5
Loaf Pan	8 × 4 × 3	1.5 L	20 × 10 × 7
	9 × 5 × 3	2 L	23 × 13 × 7
Round Layer Cake Pan	8 × 1 1/2	1.2 L	20 × 4
	9 × 1 1/2	1.5 L	23 × 4
Pie Plate	8 × 1 1/4	750 mL	20 × 3
	9 × 1 1/4	1 L	23 × 3
Baking Dish or Casserole	1 quart	1 L	—
	1 1/2 quart	1.5 L	—
	2 quart	2 L	—